# Progressiv

# Beginner
# Singing

**By**
**Peter Gelling**

**Visit our Website**
**www.learntoplaymusic.com**

      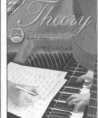

*The Progressive Series of Music Instruction Books, CDs, and DVDs*

**PROGRESSIVE BEGINNER SINGING**
**I.S.B.N. 1 864691 32 8**
**Order Code: CP-69132**

**Acknowledgments**
Cover Photograph: Phil Martin
Photographs: Phil Martin

For more information on this series contact;
L.T.P. Publishing Pty Ltd
email: info@learntoplaymusic.com
or visit our website;
**www.learntoplaymusic.com**

# Contents

# Introduction

*Progressive Beginner Singing* will give you an enjoyable and well rounded introduction to the basics of singing and reading music, as well as essential information on correct breathing and posture, how to develop your own interpretation of a song, and valuable tips on performing in public and how to use microphones. The book is suitable for anyone who wants to learn to sing. No previous musical knowledge or experience is necessary. Each new technique or note value is introduced separately and all examples sound great and are fun to sing. The book also features several well known popular songs sung in a variety of styles. On completion of the book, you will be ready to begin improvising, writing songs and playing with other musicians as well as being able to sing several popular songs and make great sounds.

The best and fastest way to learn is to use this book in conjunction with:

1.  Buying sheet music and song books of your favourite recording artists and learning to sing their songs. By learning songs, you will begin to build a repertoire and always have something to sing on social occasions or in jam sessions.

2.  Practicing and playing with other musicians. You will be surprised how good a basic melody and accompaniment can sound.

3.  Learning more about music and learning to accompany yourself on either piano, keyboard or guitar. This will help you relate to what other musicians are doing when they accompany you. It will also help you to write songs without relying on someone else to provide the musical knowledge.

4.  Learning by listening to your favourite CD's. Start building a collection of albums of singers you admire or wish to emulate. Try singing along with one of them for a short time each day. Most of the great popular singers have learned a lot of their music this way.

In the early stages it is also helpful to have the guidance of an experienced teacher. This will also help you keep to a schedule and attain weekly goals. To help you develop a good sense of time it is recommended that you **always** practice with a metronome or drum machine.

For more books and recordings by the author, visit: **www.bentnotes.com**

# How to Use the CD

Each of the musical examples and exercises in the book have been recorded on the accompanying CD. For the majority of the examples you will first hear a female voice, then a male voice, followed by a second version with no singing at all for your own practice. For each of the songs you will hear a chord played by a piano to establish the key of the song in your mind, followed by the starting note of the song. With each of the songs, only the first verse is sung on the recording. This is followed by a longer version of the song without any singing, so you can practice any or all of the verses.

Each exercise has a CD symbol next to it.

**2** ← CD Track Number

# LESSON ONE

## *Everyone Can Sing*

Everyone has a natural desire to sing. It is a way of expressing feelings and emotions as well as telling stories and reminding us of important events and times in our lives. For some the desire to sing is an instinctive personal thing and there is no wish to share the sound with others or perform. The classic example of this is singing in the shower. For others the feelings associated with singing are more significant and represent a desire to be involved in music, whether it is singing with friends, or in a choir or with a band or orchestra. Many people say they can't sing, but this is rarely true. It usually means the person is not confident about the sound of their singing voice. However, with a bit of knowledge of fundamentals like learning to sing pitches and rhythms by ear and a bit of practice, it is the author's belief that everyone can sing at least enough to gain a great deal of pleasure from it.

## **Matching Pitches and Rhythms**

Probably the most important aspect of singing is to be able to sing a given pitch accurately for a specific period of time. Many people have trouble with this at first, but it is really just a matter of **listening**, **practice** and **patience**. All notes used in music can be written down and therefore have a specific pitch and time value. Through the course of this book you will learn the fundamentals of all of the common time values for notes as well as a method of identifying pitches and how they relate to other pitches in a song. The best way to start improving your ability to sing "in time" and "in tune" is to copy the sounds made by someone else. The easiest way to do this is to sing along with a recording of one of your favorite songs and try to copy the singer. If you don't have a suitable recording, listen to the following vocal phrase on the accompanying CD and copy it. Memorise the phrase and then sing along with the CD. Don't worry about the written music for now, just copy the sounds you hear on the recording. The more you do this with songs, the easier it will get.

La      la  la  la  la        la  la  la    la   —  —  —   la

# Vocal Range

You may have noticed that on the recording, the previous example was sung first by a female voice and then by a male voice. In general, female voices are higher in pitch than male voices, although everybody's voice range is individual and there are many variations. The "range" of a persons voice is determined by the highest and lowest notes they can sing. Vocal ranges are discussed in detail in lesson 3. When you are learning to copy recorded versions of songs by ear, you may feel that you have the correct notes but your version sounds higher or lower than the one you are copying. E.g. if you are a female singer learning from a version of a song sung by a male singer, your version may be higher. This is because you have a higher voice range than the male singer. In this case you are likely to be singing the notes in a different octave to the original. An octave is a measurement of distance in music which will be explained in lesson 3.

# Timbre

If you are interested in singing, you probably have one or more favorite singers. A large part of what attracts us to a particular singer's voice is the way it sounds rather than the notes the singer uses. Every singer has an individual sound because everyone's anatomy is slightly different. Just as each person has a different height, weight, arm and leg length, coarseness or fineness of hair, skin tone etc, we all have slightly different shapes, sizes and thicknesses of the parts of the body involved in singing. The lungs, windpipe, larynx, tongue, lips, and cavities in the mouth and behind the nose are all individual and combine to create a particular **timbre** (tonal quality or tone color). All musical instruments have their own timbre which makes them easy to distinguish from one another even when they are playing exactly the same notes. Listen to the following example which is played first on the guitar and then on the flute. Although they are both playing the same notes, they are easy to tell apart because each instrument has a different timbre.

 **2**

# The Ultimate Melodic Instrument

The human voice can be thought of as the ultimate melodic instrument, because it is capable of instant expression with no instrument required to translate thoughts and feelings into sound. The voice is capable of a huge variety and depth of expressions. With the human voice, thought almost equals sound. As a baby begins to communicate with its parents and relatives, the body instinctively learns how to reproduce all the sounds of language heard by the ears and processed by the brain. Later, when the child begins to learn about language at school, vowels, consonants, words, phrases, sentences, etc. are all analysed and classified and this natural learning expands into a whole world of communication. With singing it is largely the same process. There are many different sounds used in various styles of singing, including slides, dips, growls, pure bell like tones, etc. These can all be learned simply by imitating the sounds you hear and then working at perfecting them. Many times in music, instruments imitate the human voice because of its pure expression and feeling. A classic example of this is in African American music such as Blues or Gospel, where an instrument or group of instruments answers a vocalist in a "call and response" style. This is demonstrated in the following example, where the voice is answered by the guitar. Because the human voice was used for expression before the invention of instruments and because all melodic instruments learn from the human voice, it can be said that **all music** is comes from vocal music.

 **3**

# How We Sing

The ability to sing is a by-product of the way nature has equipped the human body for speech. By simply imagining the pitch of a note, the body automatically knows how to achieve this note once the brain has issued the order to produce it. The lyrics to a song may be in any number of languages, but the pitch of a note is common to all languages. The sound which we know as singing is made primarily by air from an exhaled breath passing over the **vocal cords**, and causing them to vibrate. The vocal cords are small muscular folds of skin located inside the larynx (commonly known as the "voice box"). The sound is then amplified (made louder) and modified by the **resonance spaces** in the mouth and throat and behind the nose. The sound may also be altered by the shape of the mouth, the lips and movements of the tongue as the sound leaves the mouth. Because everybody's anatomy is slightly different, each voice will have its own individual sound both when speaking and singing.

The following diagram shows all of the parts of the body which are involved in creating the initial sound of a singing note. A singing breath usually starts with the diaphragm muscle and then travels upward from there. The air then flows over the vocal cords which are activated by a message from the brain. This produces the initial sound just as in speech. The sound then travels up into the cavities in the throat and behind the nose. These are called resonance spaces because they cause the sound to resonate, which means they reinforce and prolong the sound by vibration. These resonance spaces affect the tone of the sound and contribute to the individual sound of each person's voice. The final aspect of singing is the articulation or shaping of the sound, which is done by the tongue, throat and lips. All these things combine to form the sounds we know as singing.

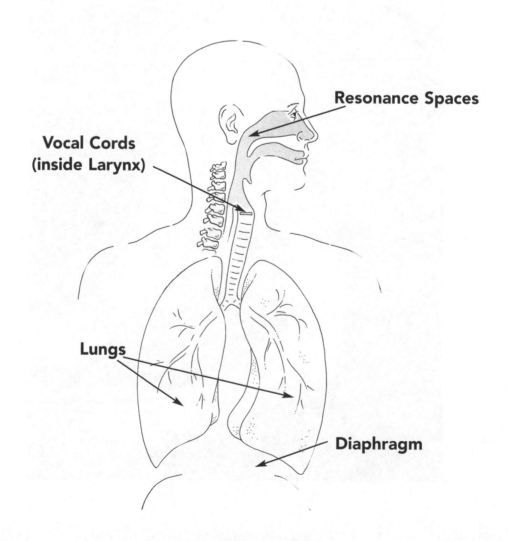

# *Breathing*

One of the most important elements of singing is a consistent and relaxed approach to breathing and breath control. A good singer always produces a strong, even tone and sounds relaxed regardless of how high or low the notes are. Outlined below is a method of breathing which will help you gain more control over the way you breathe when singing and give you a solid consistent approach which will eventually become automatic, enabling you to forget about breathing and concentrate totally on the music you are making.

A good way of developing your breathing technique is the use of visualisation. When you breathe **in**, think of an inflatable life raft which fills automatically when you pull out the plug. This will help you equate breathing in with relaxation. When you breathe **out**, think of a tube of toothpaste being slowly squeezed from the end (not the middle). This will help you use your breath economically in a controlled manner.

It is important to develop the habit of controlling your breathing from your diaphragm muscle (shown in the diagram below). As you breathe **in**, let the diaphragm relax downwards and allow the lungs to fill with air right to the bottom. Then breathe **out slowly**, squeezing gently from the diaphragm (like the tube of toothpaste) and see how long you can sustain your outgoing breath. The more control you have of your diaphrhagm, the easier you  will find breathing when you play.

1.  The more you can relax, the deeper your breath will be, and the more control you will have over it..

2.  Visualize a tube of toothpaste. Don't squeeze from the top. Gently squeeze from your abdominal area and all the air will be used and you'll have more control.

3.  Like any new habit, this method of breathing needs to be conciously worked on. Do it every day, and remember what you are trying to achieve and why.

3.  Use this breathing method even when you are not practicing. In time it will become natural and you won't have to think about it.

**Remember**
**Breathe in  =   Relax (let the lungs fill naturally**
**Blow out   =   Gentle controlled effort**

# Posture

The term "posture" refers to the way the body is held (e.g. straight, slumped, etc) and its position when sitting or standing. For singing, it is best to stand rather than sit, as this allows the most open and unrestricted passage of air for both breathing and singing. Of course, if you are accompanying yourself on piano you will have to sit. In this situation, it is essential to sit up straight but relaxed for the best sound. The best posture for singing is demonstrated in the diagram below on the right. Compare this to the incorrect posture position shown on the left.

## Incorrect

## Correct

The spine is not straight and the head and pelvis both tilt forward. In this position, it is not possible to move freely or produce the best sound.

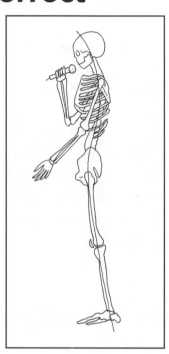

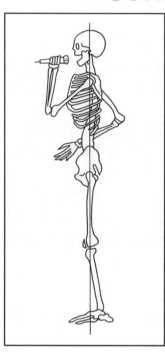

The spine is comfortably straight and in line with the head, legs and pelvis. This position keeps the airways open and makes movement easy and comfortable.

If you think of a situation where a singer is performing with a band, it would look fairly dull if the singer stood straight in the one position all the time. Movement is a large part of any stage show. This means it is not always possible for the singer to maintain perfect posture. However, it is possible to keep the pathway from the diaphragm to the mouth open, flexible and relaxed most of the time, which means it is still possible to sing well while moving around. Relaxation and flexibility are keys to good posture regardless of standing or sitting position.

# Learning to Sing

As mentioned previously, the body instinctively knows how to sing. Becoming a better singer is simply a matter of training and improving a natural process. As with any activity, there will always be some people who seem able to do it well and sound great with very little work and others who have to spend much more time developing their voice and technique, but you can be sure that all of the "great" singers you can think of in any style of music have spent many years perfecting their craft. Everyone starts with a voice, only time will tell  where it can go from there.

Although singing is a natural process, there are certain basic principles which can be applied to make the most of your particular voice. The most important of these is keeping the pathway of the voice as **open and relaxed** as possible. When you yawn, the pathway from your lungs to your lips is completely open. When singing, the mouth is not usually open as much as when yawning, but the general position and shape is the same. When forming all the different words used in speech, the position of the lips, jaw, tongue and throat will all change, but if you keep in mind that the best sounds come from an open and relaxed approach, you will be able to achieve a better singing tone regardless of the words you are singing.

# *Pre-Hearing Notes*

A second principle of good singing is to avoid straining to reach high or low notes, particularly when your voice is getting tired. If you begin learning a musical instrument, it takes time to train the muscles involved in playing that particular instrument. It is the same with singing. Singing makes use of the vocal cords which are in effect muscles inside the larynx. With practice, your range will increase and you will find it easier to sing for longer periods. The secret of reaching high and low notes is to **imagine** them before you sing them. Try to develop the ability to hear the music in your mind before you sing it. This is called **visualizing** or **pre hearing**. When you can do this, it will help you overcome reaching uncertainly for notes and will increase your general singing confidence as well as your ability.

# *Common Problems*

When children learn to read, they usually begin by reading out loud before moving on to reading silently. In the transition period, they may read to themselves but their lips still form the words as they read. After a while they progress to simply reading without moving their lips. This is a useful analogy for the process involved in learning to sing. Beginning singers instinctively move their larynx higher when singing high notes and lower when singing low notes. However, this creates tension in the throat and actually restricts the free flow of sound required for a good singing tone. When you move your larynx up or down, you are using the muscles outside the larynx instead of the vocal cords. Be aware that you will achieve a better sound by keeping your larynx stable and relaxed as you sing. Let the air and the vocal cords make the sound. Imagine the sound of the note you wish to sing and trust your body to make that sound. If it can't, the answer is patience. A beginning pianist cannot be a virtuoso in three weeks and neither can a vocalist.

Another common problem (again related to moving the lips when reading) is head movement when reaching for high or low notes. For the best sound, keep your head in the same position as you would when speaking to someone the same height as yourself. This allows the most open and relaxed pathway for your voice.

**Incorrect**
reaching for high notes

**Incorrect**
reaching for low notes

**Correct**
speech position

A third common problem which interferes with good tone is tension, particularly in the jaw. Before you sing, It is a good idea to tense your body and then let it relax. First try this with the whole body and then do it with specific areas like the shoulders, chest, throat, tongue, jaw, and face muscles.

# Registers

The singing voice is commonly divided into two **registers**. A register is a group of notes which have the same tonal characteristics. These two registers are the **chest register** (or chest voice) and the **head register** (or head voice). When you sing a low note, you can feel the vibrations in your chest and throat. When you sing a high note, you feel the vibration in the roof of your mouth and nasal area as well as your head. When singing notes in the middle of your range, you use a combination of chest voice and head voice. Some people call this another register, while others see it as a blend of the two basic registers. One of the most difficult aspects of training the voice is getting a smooth transition from one register to another. At some point there is what is commonly known as a "break", where the voice cracks or partially seizes up before moving into a new register.
You can hear this if you sing a low note and gradually slide up to a high note while sustaining the sound. The eventual aim of all singers is to overcome this break and have one big register from the bottom to the top of their range. One general principle of singing is that less air is required to make a good sound as the notes get higher. A break can be more noticeable if the sound is forced by too much air being used as the notes get higher or by straining the muscles outside the larynx.

# Working With a Teacher

To work on this aspect of singing, it is best to work with a vocal teacher. In fact, if you are serious about singing, it is strongly recommended that you work with a teacher so as to learn the best technique right from the beginning. Find a teacher who is familiar with the style of music you are most interested in singing, but also keep your mind open to other styles of music. There is much to be learned from great singers in all styles of music. Listening to great singers and imitating them is another excellent way to develop your voice, particularly by being aware of the sounds and sensations involved in making good sounds.

# Breath Control

As mentioned previously, it is common to use more air, movement and muscle activity than necessary when singing. There are two common exercises which are useful for learning to use less force and less air when singing. The first of these is to slowly blow up a balloon, using slow sustained breaths controlled from the diaphragm. The idea is to take a comfortable breath using the technique described earlier and then breathe into the balloon using an even sustained amount of air pressure. Repeat this until the balloon is full.

The second exercise is to sing in front of a lighted candle. This requires a more subtle release of air than blowing up a balloon, as the idea is to sing with as little effect on the flame of the candle as possible. Once you can sustain a note without moving the flame much, try beginning the note softly and gradually increasing the volume, then reverse the process. You could also try singing a whole verse from a song. As with all aspects of singing, be patient and you will see great improvement as long as you continue to practice.

# LESSON TWO

# Understanding Music

Although singing is a natural process, it can be improved in quality, range and accuracy of pitch and rhythm just as an instrumentalist can improve their ability with practice. Since it is the brain which issues the information for singing, it is most important to train the brain to recognise sounds and to build up a bank of knowledge which makes it easier to understand the whole process of making music. This has the added benefit of helping you to relate to what other musicians are playing and understanding the way a song's melody and its accompaniment work together, as well as making it easier to understand the sheet music of any song you wish to learn.

# How to Read Music

These five lines are called the **staff** or **stave**.

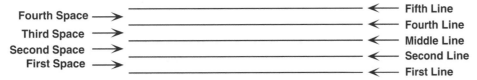

## The Treble Clef

This symbol is called a **treble clef**. There is a treble clef at the beginning of every line of most vocal sheet music.

## Music Notes

There are only seven letters used for notes in music. They are:

**A B C D E F G**

These notes are known as the **musical alphabet.**

Music notes are written in the spaces and on the lines of the treble staff.

## The Quarter Note

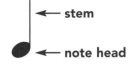

This music note is called a **quarter note**.
A quarter note lasts for **one beat**.

## The Treble Staff

A staff with a treble clef written on it is called a **treble staff**.

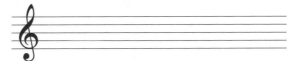

## Note and Rest Values

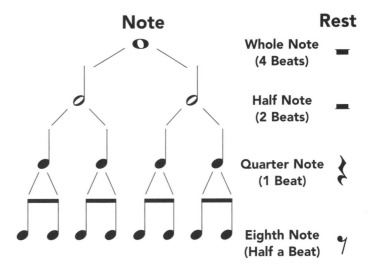

To remember the notes on the lines of the treble staff, say:
**E**very **G**ood **B**oy **D**eserves **F**ruit.

The notes in the spaces of the treble staff spell:
**F A C E**

**Bar lines** are drawn across the staff, which divides the music into sections called **Bars** or **Measures**. A **Double bar line** signifies either the end of the music, or the end of an important section of it.

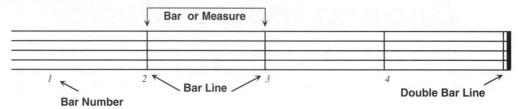

# The Four Four Time Signature

These two numbers are called the **four four time signature.**
They are placed after the treble clef.
The $\frac{4}{4}$ time signature tells you there are four beats in each bar.
There are **four** quarter notes in one bar of music in $\frac{4}{4}$ time.

The following example demonstrates two bars of quarter notes in $\frac{4}{4}$ time. In the first bar, all four notes are on the same pitch (a middle C note) while the second bar contains four notes of varying pitches. The pitch of a note has no effect on how long the note should sound, i.e. a quarter note lasts for one beat regardless of whether it is a G, C, F, or any other pitch. **The most important thing here is the rhythm.** Don't worry about the pitches too much at this stage, as singing accurate pitches from written music takes a lot of practice and is often impossible without first hearing a reference pitch from an instrument (e.g. keyboard or guitar). Listen to the example on the CD and then imitate the sounds you hear. Sing each note using the syllable **la**. Also practice reading the music and counting the rhythm out loud. Another valuable way to practice rhythms is to tap your foot and count on each beat while clapping the written rhythm.

| Sing | la | la | la | la | la | la | la | la |
| Count | 1 | 2 | 3 | 4 | 1 | 2 | 3 | 4 |

# The Half Note

This music note is called a **half note**. It has a value of **two** beats.
There are **two** half notes in one bar of $\frac{4}{4}$ time.

**Count: 1**  2

The next example contains two bars of half notes in $\frac{4}{4}$ time. To make sure you start your first note in the right place, count 1, 2, 3, 4 before starting. This will help you get the feel of the rhythm. As you proceed through the example, think -**one two** as you sing the first note in each bar and - **three four** as you sing the second note in each bar. Tap your foot on each beat to help you keep time. On the recording there are **four** drumbeats to introduce examples in $\frac{4}{4}$ time. Count along with the beats to help you establish the correct tempo (speed).

**5**

The **big** numbers **1** and **3** tell you to sing the note. The **small** numbers 2 and 4 tell you to sustain it until the next note. Notice that there are four beats in each bar. Once again, use the syllable **la** to sing this example.

**6**

Now try this one which combines half notes and quarter notes.

# When to Breathe

The previous three examples have been only two bars long. However, when you are singing a song, even one verse will be at least eight bars long. This means you will have to find places in the music where you can take a breath. A good place to breathe is at the end of a phrase (group of notes), at the end of a bar or at the end of a long note. This means that your breathing time is taking up some of the value of the note, but sometimes this is inevitable. In time you will instinctively find places to breathe which cause the least interruption to the flow of the music. Remember to breathe from the diaphragm and be careful not to lose your timing when you breathe. Counting mentally and tapping your foot on the beat as you sing should help you become more confident with this.

# The Whole Note

This is a **whole note**.
It lasts for **four** beats.
There is **one** whole note in one bar of $\frac{4}{4}$ time.

**O**

Count: **1** 2 3 4

**7**

This example is four bars long and contains whole notes in bars 2 and 4. A good place to breathe here would be at the end of each whole note. The two dots before the double bar are called a **repeat sign** and indicate that the music is to be played or sung again from the beginning.

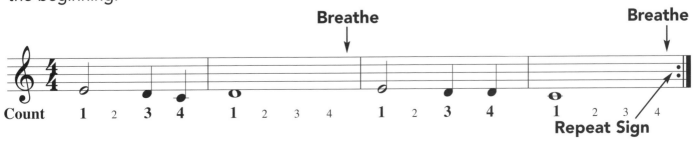

# A Word About Pitch

Although there are only seven alphabetical names used in music – **A B C D E F G** – these notes are repeated on higher and lower pitches over a large range of notes. Because everybody has a different voice range, not all singers will be comfortable with the same pitches. The actual pitch of the notes given in the examples in this book are just a guide, so if you feel comfortable singing the examples on a higher or lower pitch than the ones given here, that's fine. The important thing with these examples is to get the correct **timing**.

# Rests

Rests are used in music notation to indicate a period of silence. For every note value, there is an equivalent rest. Rests provide a natural space to take a breath as well as helping to group notes into phrases. Just as speech is organised into words, phrases and sentences, a song melody is made up of notes grouped into phrases with spaces in between them. These spaces are usually indicated by rests.

# The Half Rest

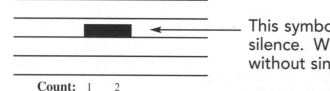

Count: 1   2

This symbol is called a **half rest**. It indicates **two** beats of silence. When you see this rest, count for **two beats** without singing.

 **8**

This example uses half notes along with half rests. In this book, **small** counting numbers are used under rests. Use the syllable "**ah**" to sing this example.

Count   **1**  2  3  4   **1**  2  3  4   1  2  **3**  4   **1**  2  3  4

# The Whole Rest

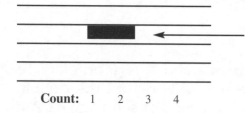

Count: 1   2   3   4

This symbol is called a **whole rest**. It indicates either **four** beats of silence or a **whole bar** of silence. The whole rest looks similar to the half rest. The difference is that the whole rest falls under the line, whereas the half rest sits on top of the next line down.

 **9**

Count   **1**  2  3  4   1  2  3  4   1  2  **3**  4   1  2  3  4

# The Quarter Rest

 This symbol is a **quarter rest.** It indicates **one beat of silence**. Do not sing any note. Remember that small counting numbers are placed under rests.

Count: 1

Count: 1

 **10**

This example contains quarter rests. Remember to **count** silently to keep time regardless of whether you see notes or rests in the music. This example is sung using the syllable "**ba**".

# The Importance of Timing

One of the most important attributes of any great singer or instrumentalist is great timing. This means they have developed the ability to begin and end a note or phrase at precisely the right moment and to fit their singing in with the accompaniment for maximum musical and dramatic effect. There are two good ways to develop your timing. One is to read rhythms from written music in time with a metronome or drum machine and the other is to have someone else play or sing rhythms and then copy them by ear. Some Rap singers are able to improvise incredibly complex and dramatic rhythms on the spot. This is called "freestyling". Even though these singers use complex rhythms, they all had to start with the same simple note values you are learning here. It is also important to remember that all music regardless of style uses the same note values. The notes are just put together in different ways to create different sounds.

Listen to the following examples on the CD to hear first the guitar and then the voice produce each short phrase. Following these, each example is repeated with the guitar playing the phrase and then a space is left for you to reproduce it with your voice. All the examples are in 4/4 time. To help keep time as you do this exercise, tap your foot in 4/4 time and remember to keep track of the beginning of each bar.

 **11. (Listen to CD)**

# LESSON THREE

## Voice Types and Ranges

The **range** of your voice is determined by the highest and lowest notes you can sing. As mentioned earlier, everybody has a different voice range. However, there are some general categories used to describe typical voice ranges. In traditional four part vocal writing, voices are broken up into four categories - **soprano** (highest female voice), **alto** (lower female voice), **tenor** (higher male voice) and **bass** (lowest male voice). When describing common voice types, these categories can be further subdivided with each of the two female and male voice types dividing into three. The three female voice types are **soprano** (highest), **mezzo soprano** (a little lower) and **alto** or **contralto** (lowest). The three male voice types are **tenor**, **baritone** and **bass**. The middle voices (mezzo soprano and baritone) are the most common voices. Another unusual voice type is the male alto. All of these voice types are descriptions of adult voices. Children and teenagers have voices which are not fully developed, so they cannot be classified as a final voice type. It is a good idea to find out what your range is as soon as you understand how to find the notes on a keyboard. However, it is unwise to classify yourself immediately as any particular voice type. It is always best to consult a singing teacher and work with them for a while before classifying a voice accurately. Male voices reach their eventual range later than female voices, so young male students may not be able to classify their voice type until they are adults. The most important thing is to know your individual note range and work with it rather than against it by straining to sing higher or lower than is practical for you.

## How to Find Your Voice Range

The easiest way to find the highest and lowest notes in your range is to test them against a piano or keyboard. Even if you don't intend to play any instrument, it is important to understand the layout of a keyboard in order to identify notes and understand the relationship between them. A keyboard is tuned to concert pitch, which is an international standard for identifying notes. This enables musicians in bands and orchestras to play in tune with each other. When you sing, your perception of pitch may change depending on your state of mind or how tired you are. For this reason, it is important to have a reference from a fixed pitch instrument tuned to concert pitch.

## The Keyboard

The black keys always appear in groups of two or three. The note **C** is often the starting note for relating all other notes to. The **C note** is a **white key**. It is always on the left hand side of a group of two black keys. The C note in the middle of the keyboard is called middle C. This note is in the range of all of the voice types, although it will be towards the top of some male voice ranges and towards the bottom of some female voice ranges.

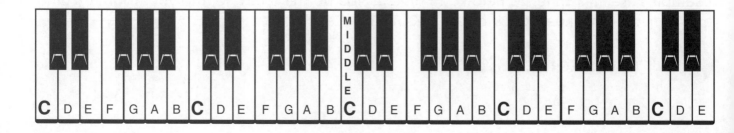

## The Bass Clef

This symbol is called a **bass clef**. Vocal music for tenor, baritone and bass voices usually uses a bass clef instead of a treble clef.

## The Bass Staff

A staff with a bass clef written on it is called a **bass staff**.

# The Grand Staff

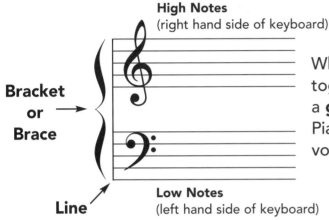

**High Notes**
(right hand side of keyboard)

**Bracket or Brace** →

**Line** ↗

**Low Notes**
(left hand side of keyboard)

When the treble and bass staves are joined together by a line and a bracket, they are called a **grand staff**.

Piano music is written on the grand staff. Four part vocal music can also be written on the grand staff.

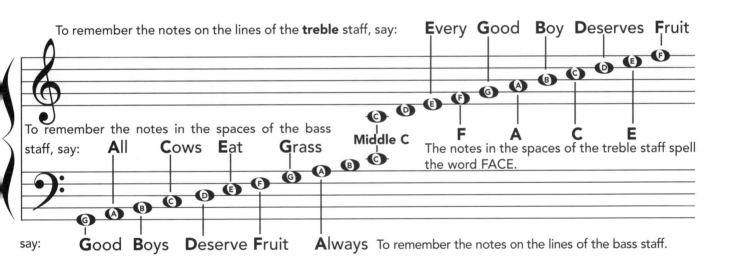

To remember the notes on the lines of the **treble** staff, say: **Every Good Boy Deserves Fruit**

To remember the notes in the spaces of the bass staff, say: **All Cows Eat Grass**

Middle C

The notes in the spaces of the treble staff spell the word FACE.

**F A C E**

say: **Good Boys Deserve Fruit Always** To remember the notes on the lines of the bass staff.

**Middle C** is written just **below** the **treble** staff or just **above** the **bass** staff on a short line called a **leger** line. Any other notes above or below a staff are also written on leger lines.

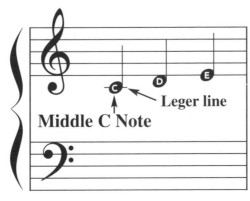

**Middle C Note**

**Leger line**

The following keyboard diagrams show typical ranges of the six basic voice types. Remember that everyone's voice range is individual and that your own voice may fall between any of the traditional categories. Another important thing to keep in mind is that these are voice ranges of fully developed singing voices, so your voice when you start learning to sing may have a smaller range than the ones shown here. Many tenors have larger ranges than the one shown here. Listen to the CD to hear the highest and lowest notes of each range.

 **12.0**                        **Soprano**

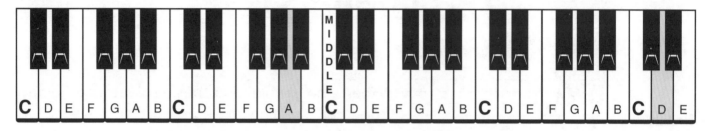

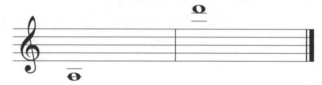

 **12.1**                  **Mezzo Soprano**

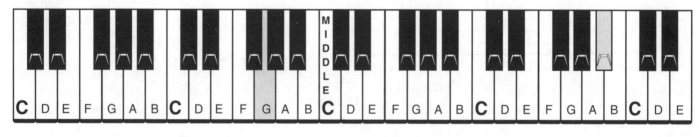

 **12.2**                        **Alto**

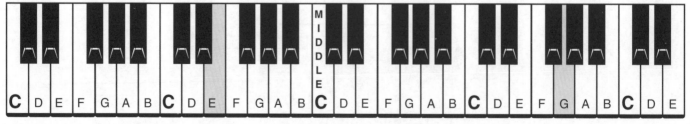

**12.3**                    **Tenor**

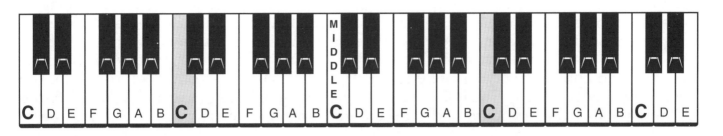

**12.4**                    **Baritone**

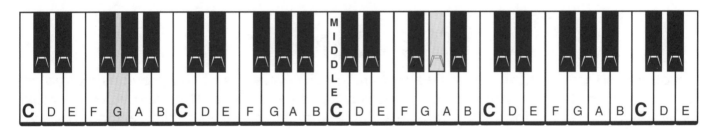

**12.5**                    **Bass**

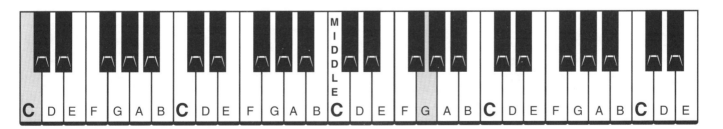

# Matching Pitches

One of the most important aspects of singing is the ability to sing any desired pitch accurately. A good way to develop your pitching ability (called **intonation**) is to play or have someone else play notes on an instrument (e.g. keyboard) and copy the pitches with your voice. Some people find this easy immediately while others have to work at it for a while before they can do it. The most important thing is to listen carefully to the pitch being played and to trust your body to be able to produce that pitch. Relax and let the sound come out naturally. The following examples demonstrate this exercise. Listen to the CD to hear first the keyboard and then the voice produce each pitch. Following these, each example is repeated with the keyboard playing the pitch and then a space is left for you to reproduce the pitch with your voice. All of the examples are in ⁴⁄₄ time. Each pitch is a half note (two beats) on the first beat of the bar. The final two beats of each bar are a half note rest. Each pitch is sung with the syllable "**la**".

**13.  Female**

**14.  Female Practice**

**15.  Male**

**16.  Male Practice**

# The Octave

If you listen through both the male and female voice versions of the previous examples, you will notice that the sequence of notes is relatively the same. The male voice example is simply a lower version of the female voice example. These examples are one **octave** apart. Although there are only seven different letter names used in music - A, B, C, D, E, F and G - there are various repetitions of these note names at higher and lower pitches. E.g. the following example demonstrates all the natural notes from **A** in the bottom space of the bass staff to **A** on the first leger line above the treble staff. This covers a range of **three octaves**. Every time you come to a new A note after going through all the other letter names, the new **A** note is in a new octave. Proceeding through all the other pitches, each of them is one octave above the previous note with the same name. For example, middle **C** is one octave above the **C** in the second bottom space of the bass staff, the **F** in the bottom space of the treble staff is one octave below the **F** on the top line of the treble staff, etc. This is easy to understand by looking at the keyboard.

**17**

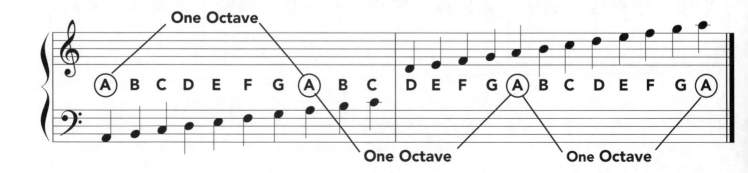

# LESSON FOUR

## *The Major Scale*

Most melodies are derived from **scales**. A scale is a pattern of notes at different pitches, which can be repeated in higher or lower registers and sung or played on any melodic instrument. Apart from vocal melodies, most bass lines and lead solos are also made up of notes from scales. A scale may start on any pitch and the name of the starting note of the scale determines the name of the scale. The most common building block for melodies is the **major scale**. The simplest of these is the **C major scale**, which starts and ends on the note **C** and contains all of the natural notes used in music.

A major scale is a group of eight notes that produces the familiar sound:

**Do Re Mi Fa So La Ti Do**

In the **C major scale**, these sounds are represented by the notes:

**C    D    E    F    G    A    B    C**

On the keyboard, the C major scale represents all the white notes, beginning and ending on C in any octave.

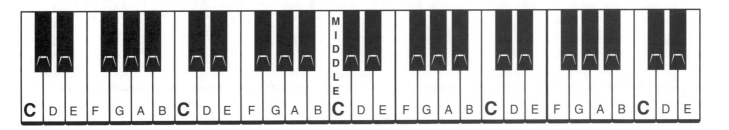

The following example demonstrates the C major scale sung by both female (treble staff) and male (bass staff) voices. Sing along with the one which best suits your voice range. The first note and last note of a major scale always have the same name. In the **C major** scale the distance from the lowest C to the C note above it is one octave. This example is one octave of the C major scale. Each of the voices is also one octave apart.

 **18**

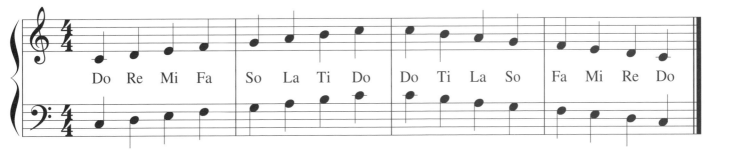

Do Re Mi Fa | So La Ti Do | Do Ti La So | Fa Mi Re Do

The major scale is built up from a pattern of two types of **intervals** (distances between notes). These intervals are called the tone (indicated by **T**) and the semitone (indicated by **S**). A semitone is the smallest interval used in western music. Notes which are a tone apart leave room for other notes between them. These in between notes are called **sharps** and **flats** which are discussed in the following lesson. The numbers under the letter names are **scale degrees** which indicate the position of each note in the scale.

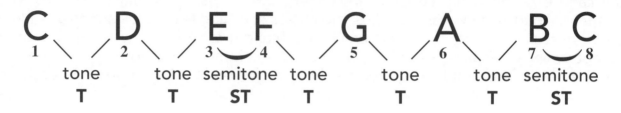

On the keyboard, the distance between one key and the key directly next to it on either side is a semitone. Keys a semitone apart are usually one black and one white key, except for E to F and B to C which are semitones involving two white keys. Working out the distance of a whole tone is easy as it is simply two semitones. As you can see from the C major scale above, all other white key notes apart from E to F and B to C are a whole tone apart.

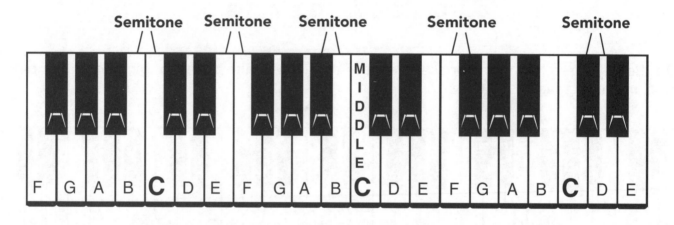

# Octave Displacement

Here is a short melody created from the C major scale. Many of the melodies you already know will use notes derived from the major scale. This example is written on the treble staff only. Male singers can sing the same melody one octave lower at the same pitch as the male singer on the CD (second time through). This is called octave displacement, and can be indicated in written music by the symbol *8vb* which indicates that the part is to be sung or played an octave lower than written, or *8va* which indicates an octave higher than written.

**19    (Male Voice *8vb*)**

# Sol-fa Syllables

Written below are several short exercises which should help you become more familiar with the sounds which can be derived from the major scale. Each of them uses the syllables **do**, **re**, **mi**, **fa**, **so**, **la**, **ti**, and **do** again. These are called **sol-fa syllables**. They are useful for becoming familiar with all the pitches of a major scale, and their positions in relation to the foundation note of the scale (**do**). The sol-fa syllables are also useful for practicing many of the basic sounds used in singing. As you sing each of these exercises, remain as relaxed as possible and sing with an open flowing sound. Keep your posture straight and focus your voice straight ahead as if you were singing into a microphone at a comfortable height. Do not "reach" for any of the notes as they get higher or lower, but simply allow the sounds to come out naturally. You may not be able to sing these exercises easily to begin with. Be patient and practice them regularly, but only for short periods of time at each session. There are three ways to learn these exercises.

1  Sing from the written music. This is called **sight singing** and takes quite a while to develop. To learn to sight sing well, it is best to work with a teacher.

2  Sing from the sol-fa syllables. You have probably heard them before and may find them a useful guide to the pitch of each note relative to **do**.

3  Listen to the recording and imitate the pitches until you have them all memorized.

# The Three Four Time Signature

**3/4** This time signature is called the **three four** time signature. It tells you there are **three** beats in each bar. Three four time is also known as waltz time. There are **three** quarter notes in one bar of time. The following example is in ¾ time and is sung using sol-fa syllables.

 **24**

# The Dotted Half Note

Count: 1  2  3

A **dot** written after a note extends its value by **half**.
A dot after a half note means that you hold it for **three** beats.
One dotted half note makes one bar of music in ¾ time.

**25**

Here is a typical example of the way dotted half notes are used in ¾ time. Go through and work out the sol-fa syllable for each note of the melody. If you have trouble keeping accurate time while you are singing, try clapping the rhythms while counting the beats out loud and tapping your foot. This is a great way to practice any rhythm you have trouble with. The letters and numbers written above the music (**C, Em**, etc) are **chord symbols** which relate to what the accompanying instruments are playing. Chords will be discussed in lesson 9. This example is sung using the syllable **la**.

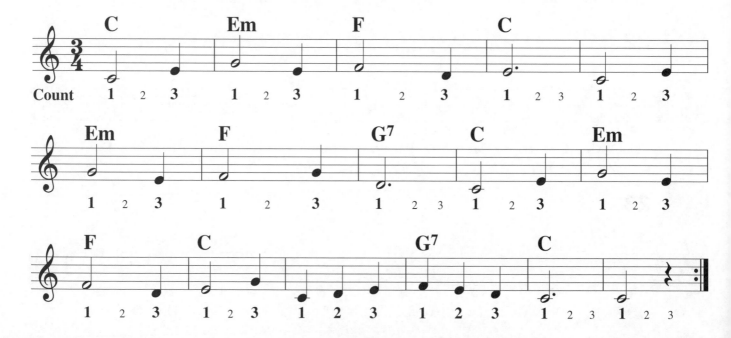

# The Eighth Note

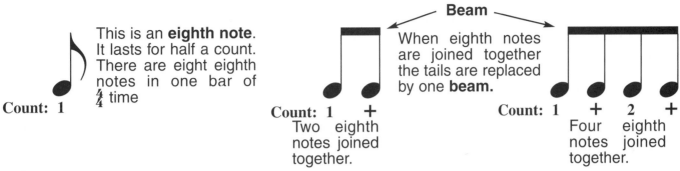

This is an **eighth note**. It lasts for half a count. There are eight eighth notes in one bar of 4/4 time

**Beam**

When eighth notes are joined together the tails are replaced by one **beam.**

Count: 1 +
Two eighth notes joined together.

Count: 1 + 2 +
Four eighth notes joined together.

 **26  How to Count Eighth Notes**

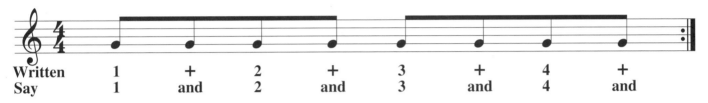

| Written | 1 | + | 2 | + | 3 | + | 4 | + |
| Say | 1 | and | 2 | and | 3 | and | 4 | and |

 **27**

This example contains some common groupings of eighth notes, along with all the other note values you have learnt. Clap the rhythms with your hands before singing this example and remember to count and tap your foot. Next, sing through the example using the syllable **la**.

## The Dotted Quarter Note

A dot written after a quarter note means that you hold the note for **one and a half beats**.

A dotted quarter note is often followed by an eighth note.

Count 1  2  +

 **28**

Once you understand some of the basic concepts of how music is written, it becomes a lot easier to understand sheet music. Written below is the song **Silent Night**, which contains many of the things you have learnt up to this point. It is in ¾ time and the melody is made up of half notes, quarter notes and eighth notes, as well as dotted half notes and dotted quarter notes. The final bar contains a whole rest which represents a full bar rest when used in ¾ time. The song is made up entirely of notes from the major scale. At this stage, you may not be able to read all the individual pitches of the notes from the written music, so sing the melody by ear but pay close attention to the timing of the notes. If you have trouble, listen to the CD and watch the written music as you listen. Count along with the music as you hear it. On the recording you will hear a second voice in the background singing a different line to the melody. This is called a **harmony**.

On the recording you will also hear a piano playing a chord and then a note before the count-in to the song begins. This is to establish the sound of the key in your mind and give you the starting pitch before you begin singing. The chord is a **C chord** which establishes the sound for the **key of C major**. The note following the chord is a **G note**, which is the **starting note** of the song. As you hear the **C** chord, think **do** in your mind, then as you hear the **G** note, think **so**. This process will happen with all the songs on the recording. When you sing with other musicians, get one of them to play the chord which establishes the key and then the starting note before you count the song in. This way you will always be confident of starting on the correct pitch and will easily hear its relationship to the key note (**do**).

 **29    Silent Night**

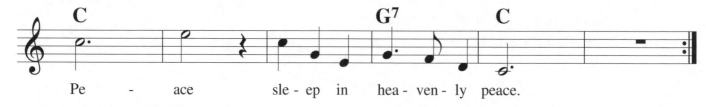

2. Silent night, holy night,
   Shepherds quake at the sight;
   Glories stream from heaven afar,
   Heavenly hosts sing Alleluia:
   Christ the Saviour is born!
   Christ the Saviour is born!

3. Silent night, holy night,
   Son of God, love's pure light;
   Radiance beams from Thy holy face,
   With the dawn of redeeming grace,
   Jesus, Lord, at Thy birth.
   Jesus, Lord, at Thy birth.

# LESSON FIVE

## Sounds Used in Singing

Like speech, the basic sounds used in singing fall into two categories – vowels and consonants. The vowels are all open sounds which flow uninterrupted from the vocal cords out through the mouth. Each vowel is given its particular sound by the shape of the mouth. Consonants, on the other hand, are sounds which interrupt the flow of air produced by a vowel sound. Consonants are articulated by the lips, front, middle or back of the tongue, and even the throat. In general, the vowels are the long or sustained sounds in singing and the consonants are kept as short as possible.

# Vowels

In spoken language, the five basic vowels are **E, A, I, O** and **U**. In singing these are modified to the sounds **EE, AY, AH, OH** and **OO**. Run through these sounds several times on one pitch and become aware of the way the shape of your mouth and position of your lips changes as you move from one sound to the next. As you sing these sounds, your tongue should remain relaxed in the bottom of your mouth and your jaw should also remain relaxed. Aim for an "open" sound and feeling as you sing each vowel. Once you are comfortable with all the sounds on a single pitch, try the following exercise which descends through the major scale. It is important to do this exercise slowly at first.

 **30**

ee ay ah oh oo     ee ay ah oh oo     ee ay ah oh oo     ee ay ah oh oo

ee ay ah oh oo     ee ay ah oh oo     ee ay ah oh oo     ee ay ah oh oo

# Dipthongs

Some words consist of two successive vowel sounds within one syllable. These vowels are called **diphthongs** With all dipthongs, the vowel starts with one sound and ends with another.

**"AH"** + **"EE"** as in Might,

**"OH"** + **"EE"** as in Noise

**"EH"** + **"EE"** as in Pain and Weight

Examples of Diphthongs:

You should attempt to keep the vowel as natural sounding as possible, letting the second sound flow out of the first. Do not over emphasise the second sound of the vowel, simply allow it to disappear naturally.

# The Shaping of Vowels

The following photos demonstrate basically the way your mouth should look when singing the five common vowel sounds. If you follow these guidelines you will achieve the purest sound with each vowel. Try practicing your vowels in front of a mirror to ensure that you develop the habit of using the correct mouth shapes.

### EE

As in "Meet": Do not allow your mouth to spread sideways, as this will produce extra tension. Your tongue should be resting comfortably on the back of your bottom teeth, but will arch slightly forward.

### AY

As in "Gate": This vowel is sometimes pronounced as a diphthong, because the vowel starts with one sound and ends with another (**EH-EE**). Keep the tongue resting on the bottom of the mouth and the jaw relaxed.

### AH

As in the expression "Ah": Try not to force this vowel. The sound should come from low in your throat. This is an excellent vowel to for practicing scales and exercises, as it allows for a very open relaxed pathway and doesn't put tension on the larynx.

### OH

As in "Coat": Allow the jaw to drop naturally and keep the mouth relaxed and in a similar position to the **AH** vowel. The lips should move forward and the inside of the mouth should feel open.

### OO

As in "Room": The lips should form an oval shape. Once again, the jaw should be relaxed and the tongue should sit comfortably on the bottom of the mouth.

# Consonants

Consonants are letters other than vowels. They are the sounds that define words and are articulated by the **lips**, **teeth**, **tongue**, **soft palette** and occasionally, the **throat**. Consonants actually interrupt the smooth, natural flow of the vowels but are very important to a singer's craft as they provide the focus for words and shape them so that they are understandable to an audience.

As a general rule, consonants should not be over-emphasised. Whereas vowels will open the vocal passages, consonants will close or restrict the free flow of air. Therefore, when singing a verse or phrase, concentrate on reproducing full, open vowel sounds while only lightly articulating the consonants.

A good way to work on consonants is to take a particular consonant and follow it with each of the vowel sounds as shown in the example below. Gradually work your way through all the consonants in the alphabet using this technique. Be aware of whether it is the lips, teeth, tongue, throat or soft palate (or combination of these) which articulate each consonant. For example, **B** and **M** involve the lips, **K** involves the soft palette, **S** and **T** involve both the tongue and teeth, **G** involves the throat and soft palette, and **J** involves all areas involved in articulating consonants. Once again, remember that when singing the main emphasis is usually on the vowel sound and that consonants are only lightly articulated so as to express the words without sounding harsh or restricting the air flow more than necessary.

 **31**

There are occasions in both speech and singing where a sound is made up of two consonants in a row, e.g. sh (as in "shot"), ng (as in "song"), or ch (as in "chew"). Like single consonants, it is worth practicing these sounds along with vowels in the manner shown above, always remembering to keep the emphasis on the vowels.

# Dynamics

The term **dynamics** refers to the volume at which music is played or sung. If all music was played at the same volume it would lack expression and become boring. Therefore it is necessary to be able to sing at a variety of dynamic levels ranging from very soft to very loud. There are particular markings for dynamics in written music. Some of these are listed below.

*pp*   very quiet      *p*   quiet      *mp*   moderately quiet

*mf*   moderately loud      *f*   loud      *ff*   very loud

Two other symbols used to indicate dynamics are the **crescendo** (meaning a gradual increase in volume) and the **diminuendo** (meaning a gradual decrease in volume). These are shown below.

**crescendo**        **diminuendo**

To begin using dynamics in your singing, there are several useful exercises you can do. One is to apply the crescendo and diminuendo to a single note while maintaining an even tone, as demonstrated in the following example. Listen to the CD if you are not sure how this should sound.

 **32**

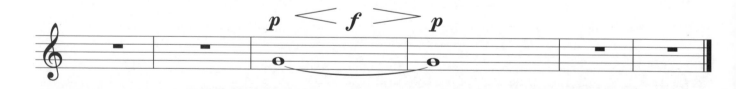

Another useful exercise is to apply the same dynamics to a major scale, i.e. sing **do** softly and gradually increase the volume as you ascend through the scale until you are singing loudly by the time you reach the **do** an octave above. Then do the same thing as you descend the scale. Next try starting loudly and get softer with each syllable until you reach the end of the scale.

The final step in adding dynamics to your singing is to apply them to a song. This is a much more personal thing and also depends on the lyrics you are trying to bring meaning to. Obviously some lyrics call for a quiet, subtle approach while others need a strong emphasis. Listen to recordings of your favorite singers and pay particular attention to the way they use dynamics. If you are singing with an accompanist or a band, you will need to rehearse your dynamics with them so that the music can "rise and fall as one". When this happens, it feels great as well as giving the ensemble the ability to move an audience more intensely.

# Slurs

**Slurs** are markings in music which indicate that successive notes are to be sung or played with only the first note being articulated. This is very common in singing where two or more notes may occur while singing a single syllable. An example is shown below. The syllable **ah** is sung on two consecutive notes, and is articulated on each note. **Ah** is then sung again, covering the same two notes but only articulated on the first note. The curved line joining the two notes indicates a slur. In the third bar, **ah** is sung again but this time covering three different notes. Once again the syllable is only articulated on the first note. When singing, slurs can be thought of as "sliding" or "gliding" between notes.

 **33**

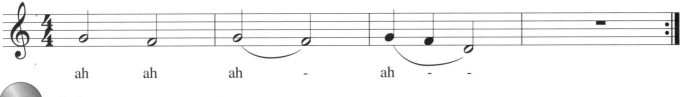

ah    ah    ah  -    ah  -  -

 **34**

A good example of the way this occurs in a song is the opening phrase of **Silent Night** which you learnt in the previous lesson. It is shown below with slur markings. To keep the music looking as simple as possible, slur markings are often left out of sheet music. You can usually tell where slurs occur because there will be more than one note for a syllable with a small horizontal line written between the lyrics (e.g. **Si - lent night**).

Si - lent  night,    Ho - ly  night,    All  is  calm,

# Phrasing and Expression

Apart from the actual notes and words used, a large part of the feeling and meaning of a song is conveyed by the particular expressions, inflections and phrasing that individual singers use. This is a very personal thing which is made up from the way the singer thinks about the song and how it relates to their own musical taste and experience of life. This is why two singers can sing the same song and produce dramatically different versions.

The term "phrasing" refers to the individual grouping of notes and/or lyrics and where punctuations and emphasis are placed. As in speech, this can alter either the actual meaning of the words or the feeling it conveys to a listener. Written below are two different ways of delivering the same set of words.

1.  (angrily)        "**<u>You</u> did it,  you <u>know</u> you did.**"

2.  (enthusiastic and complimentary)        "**You <u>did</u> it you know,  you <u>did</u>.**"

When singing any song, it is important to think about phrasing so as to be able to communicate fully with the listener and bring your own interpretation to each set of lyrics. Instrumental musicians are also aware of the power of lyrics and vocal phrasing. Many improvising musicians strive to achieve a "vocal" style of phrasing when they play. The great Jazz saxophonist Lester Young once said that he would never improvise on a song he didn't know the words to.

# Moving Between Registers

One of the most difficult aspects of singing is achieving an even tone when moving between low and high registers. Most mature voices have a vocal range of about 2 octaves (approximately 13 or 14 white notes on the keyboard). The eventual aim of a singer should be to have the lowest notes of the chest voice up to the highest notes of the head voice connected in a smooth, even manner. When moving from high notes to low notes and back again, many singers have one or more notes near the middle of their range that require(s) practice to develop an even tone. As mentioned earlier, this is called the **break**.

A good way to work at reducing the effect and severity of a break is to practice slurring from one octave of a note up to the next octave of that note and back down again to the original note. This is demonstrated in the following example, which begins on a C note and glides up to another C note an octave above before falling back to the first C note. This pattern then continues up a semitone on a C♯ note, then a D note, and so on up to a G note. This example is not notated, so you will need to listen to the CD to learn it. If some notes feel too high or too low for your voice, start and finish on whatever notes feel most appropriate for you. As you move through the different pitches, try to keep each note at the same volume and tone as the preceding ones. Work on this exercise for short periods and remember to stop if you feel you are straining your voice.

**35.   Female**     **36.   Female Practice**

**37.   Male**     **38.   Male Practice**

# Vibrato

Another expressive technique which is common to both singers and instrumentalists is **vibrato**. This is a method of altering the quality of a note once it has been sounded. It generally occurs on longer sustained notes and can be heard as a slight wavering of the pitch and volume of a note, that may be fast, slow or anywhere in between. The speed and width of vibrato are a matter of personal taste and often depend on the musical situation. There are several methods of producing vibrato with the voice. These involve movement of the diaphragm, the throat and the larynx in various combinations. The easiest way to begin developing vibrato is to imagine you are your favorite singer and to imitate the sound of their vibrato. It is a good idea to exaggerate at first, but once you have control of it, don't forget to ease off, as singers who over-use vibrato can be very irritating.

Vibrato is a very personal thing and can add a lot of character and warmth to your voice but it may take some time to develop. It is probably a good idea to work with a teacher when you are learning vibrato, as it can be difficult to obtain a good sound at first. One of the most important aspects of learning is **listening**. You can learn a lot about vibrato by simply listening to singers you admire and imitating their sound. By this stage in your development, you should be listening to albums featuring great singing every day. Listen to the following example on the CD to hear the effect of vibrato and then try it yourself. The note begins with no vibrato and the vibrato is added while the note sustains.

**39**

Gradually add vibrato

# LESSON SIX

## Sharps (♯) and Flats (♭)

Although there are only seven letter names used in music, there are actually **twelve** different notes used in music. The extra notes fall in between some of the letter names. These notes are indicated by the use of **sharps and flats**. A sharp is indicated by the symbol ♯ and means that the pitch is **raised by a semitone**. E.g. the note **C sharp** (**C♯**) is higher than C and falls halfway between the notes C and D. A flat is indicated by the symbol ♭ and means that the pitch is **lowered by a semitone**. E.g. the note **D♭** is lower than D and falls halfway between D and C. This means that the notes **C♯** and **D♭** are exactly the same. This may seem confusing but is easy to understand if you look at the piano keyboard shown in the diagram below. The white notes are all the natural notes (**A B C D E F G**) and the black notes are the sharps and flats. D♯ is the same as E♭, F♯ is the same as G♭, etc. Sometimes one is used and sometimes the other, depending on the musical situation and the **key** the music is written in. Keys are discussed on the following page.

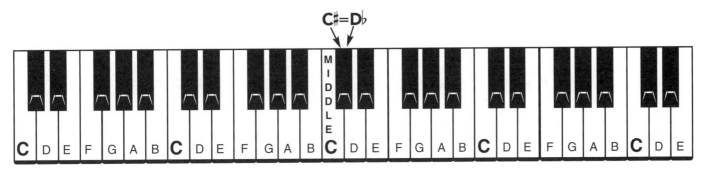

## The Chromatic Scale

As mentioned earlier, with the inclusion of sharps and flats, there are 12 different notes within one octave. The notes **EF** and **BC** are always one **semitone** apart. All the other natural notes are a **tone** apart. Sharps (♯) and flats (♭) are found between the notes that are a tone apart. If you combine all the natural notes with the sharps and flats found in between them, you end up with what is called the **chromatic scale**. This scale contains all the notes used in music. The chromatic scale is made up of twelve consecutive semitones.

$$C \quad \frac{C\sharp}{D\flat} \quad D \quad \frac{D\sharp}{E\flat} \quad EF \quad \frac{F\sharp}{G\flat} \quad G \quad \frac{G\sharp}{A\flat} \quad A \quad \frac{A\sharp}{B\flat} \quad BC$$

## Intervals

An **interval** is the distance between any two notes. Intervals are named in numbers which are larger or smaller depending on how many letter names apart the notes are. E.g. C to D is the interval of a second (C=1, D=2), C to E is the interval of a third (C D E = 1 2 3), C to F is the interval of a fourth, etc. There are actually various different types of intervals (major, minor, etc) but an in-depth study of intervals is beyond the scope of this book. At this stage it is enough to be aware that different notes can be specific distances apart based on their letter names and the number of semitones between them, and that these distances are called intervals. If you wish to pursue music more seriously, it is important to understand and be able to hear all the different intervals. Any good vocal or instrumental teacher will be able to help you with this.

# Keys

The **key** describes the note around which a piece of music is built. When a song consists of notes from a particular scale, it is said to be written in the **key** which has the same notes as that scale. For example, if a song contains mostly notes from the **C major scale**, it is said to be in the **key of C major**. If a song contains mostly notes from the **F major scale**, it is said to be in the **key of F major**. If a song contains mostly notes from the **G major scale**, it is said to be in the **key of G major**. When singing or playing in any major key other than C, the key will contain at least one sharp or flat, and possibly as many as six. Instead of writing these sharps or flats before each note as they occur, they are usually written at the beginning of the song just before the time signature. These sharps or flats are called a **key signature**. The number of sharps or flats in the key signature depends on the number of sharps or flats in the corresponding major scale. The major scales and key signatures for the keys of **F** and **G** are shown below. Without sharps and flats, these scales would not contain the correct pattern of tones and semitones and would therefore not sound like a major scale. Sol-fa syllables can be applied to any major scale. You simply call the first note of the scale do, and follow the pattern through the rest of the scale. In the key of **G major**, the note **G** would be **do**, **A** would be **re**, **B** would be **mi**, etc. In the key of **F major**, the note **F** would be **do**, **G** would be **re**, **A** would be **mi**, etc.

## G Major Scale

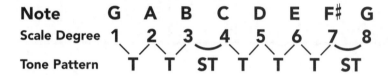

## Key Signature of G Major

The **G major** scale contains one sharp, F♯, therefore the key signature for the key of **G major** contains one sharp, F♯.

## F Major Scale

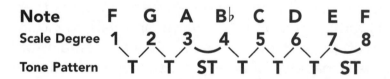

## Key Signature of F Major

The **F major** scale contains one flat, B♭, therefore the key signature for the key of **F major** contains one flat, B♭.

The reason some scales contain sharps while others contain flats is that there has to be a separate letter name for each note in the scale. E.g. the G major scale contains F♯ instead of G♭ even though these two notes are identical in sound. However, if G♭ was used, the scale would contain two notes with the letter name G and no note with the letter name F. This is the reason for choosing to call the note F♯ in this key. In the key of F major, the note B♭ is chosen instead of A♯ for the same reason. If A♯ was used, the scale would contain two notes with the letter name A and no note with the letter name B. The note each major scale starts on will determine how many sharps or flats are found in each key signature because of the necessity for the scale to have the correct pattern of tones and semitones in order to sound right. The following chart contains the key signatures of all the major scales used in music, along with the number of sharps or flats contained in each key. Because there are 12 notes used in music, this means there are 12 possible starting notes for major scales (including sharps and flats). This means that some of the keys will have sharps or flats in their name, e.g. F♯ major, B♭ major, E♭ major, etc. Keys which contain sharps are called sharp keys and keys which contain flats are called flat keys.

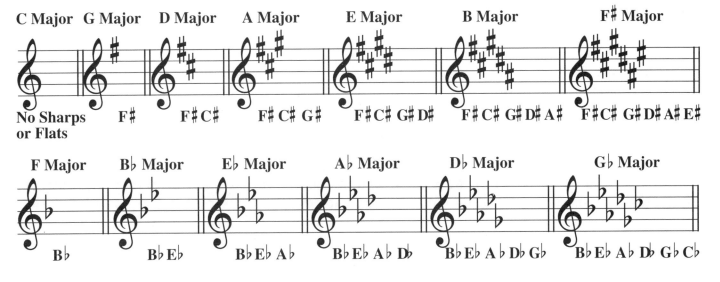

# Relative Minor Keys

So far, everything has been discussed in terms of **major** keys. However, there is another common type of key called a **minor key**. Minor keys are derived from **minor scales**. There are various different kinds of minor scales, each based on a different pattern of tones and semitones. The type of minor scale which is used to determine key signatures for minor keys is called the **natural minor scale**. For every major scale there is a **relative minor scale** which is based upon the **6th note** of the major scale. This means that if you sing the C major scale starting and finishing on **A** (A B C D E F G A) instead of C, it becomes the **A natural minor scale**. Therefore, these two scales contain exactly the same notes, but in a different order. Listen to the recording of the example below to hear the sound of the natural minor scale. Minor keys are often described as having a "sadder" sound than major keys.The chart following this example shows the relative minor of all twelve major keys.

🔘 **40**

| MAJOR KEY (I) | C | D♭ | D | E♭ | E | F | F♯ | G♭ | G | A♭ | A | B♭ | B |
|---|---|---|---|---|---|---|---|---|---|---|---|---|---|
| RELATIVE MINOR KEY (VI) | Am | B♭m | Bm | Cm | C♯m | Dm | D♯m | E♭m | Em | Fm | F♯m | Gm | G♯m |

Both the major and the relative minor share the same key signature, as shown below.

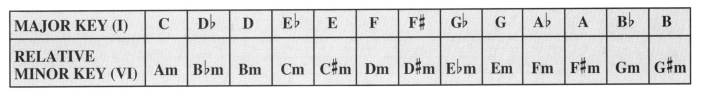

C major(I) or A minor(VI)   G major(I) or E minor(VI)   D major(I) or B minor(VI)   A major(I) or F♯ minor(VI)   E major(I) or C♯ minor(VI)   B major(I) or G♯ minor(VI)   F♯ major(I) or D♯ minor(VI)

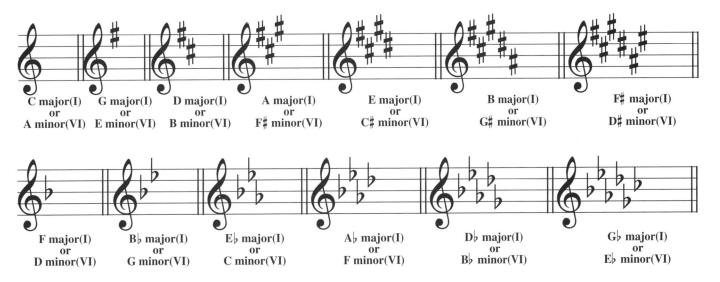

F major(I) or D minor(VI)   B♭ major(I) or G minor(VI)   E♭ major(I) or C minor(VI)   A♭ major(I) or F minor(VI)   D♭ major(I) or B♭ minor(VI)   G♭ major(I) or E♭ minor(VI)

# 41 Scarborough Fair

**Scarborough Fair** is an example of a song in a minor key. Because there is no key signature written at the start of the song, it can be seen that the song is in either C major or A minor. It is usually possible to tell which of two possible keys (major or relative minor) a song is in by looking at the note on which the melody ends, and often the starting note as well. This melody begins and ends on the note A, so this tells us that the key is A minor. Another indication is the chords which accompany the melody. The first and last chord symbol here is **Am** which indicates an A minor chord. Notice also the use of the note F sharp (**F#**) in this song. Another interesting feature of this melody is the use of the **tie**, which is a curved line connecting two notes of the same pitch. A tie indicates that you sing the first note and hold it for the value of the second note as well. Ties are discussed further in the following lesson.

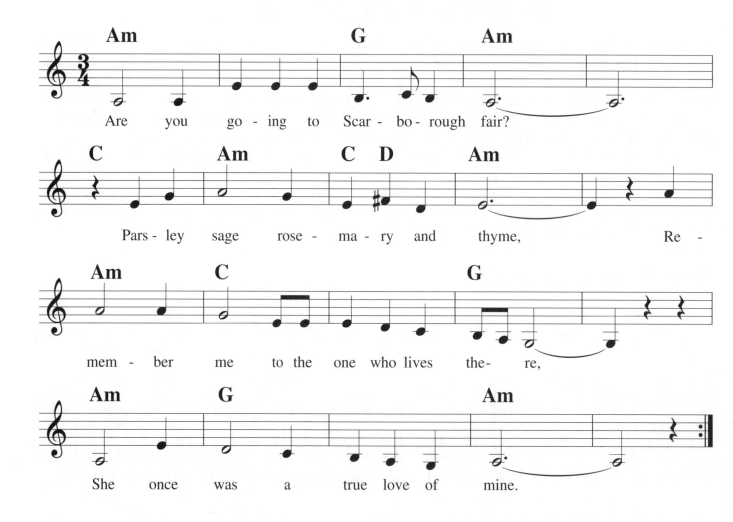

2. "Tell her to make me a cambric shirt,"
   Parsley, sage, rosemary, and thyme;
   "Without any seam or needlework,
   For once she was a true love of mine."

3. "Tell her to wash it in yonder well,"
   Parsley, sage, rosemary and thyme;
   "Where never spring water nor rain ever fell,
   For once she was a true love of mine."

4. "Now he has asked me questions three,"
   Parsley, sage, rosemary and thyme;
   "I hope he will answer as many for me,
   For once he was a true love of mine."

5. "Tell him to find me an acre of land,"
   Parsley, sage, rosemary and thyme;
   "Betwixt the salt water and the sea sand,
   For once he was a true love of mine."

**42    Scarborough Fair**

The recording contains two versions of the song **Scarborough Fair**, the first one sung by a female vocalist and the second by a male vocalist. The second version is in the key of **C minor**, as can be seen from the key signature (3 flats). A different key was chosen because it was easier for our male vocalist to sing the song in this key. As mentioned earlier, everybody has a different voice range, so many people will prefer to sing any given song in one key while many others will prefer to sing in a different key. The key chosen depends on the range of notes used in that particular melody and whether they feel comfortable for the singer. Often (e.g. in a choir) many different singers, both male and female will sing a song in the same key in unison or harmony in different octaves. The vocal exercises in this book are sung by male and female voices in the same key, but in different octaves. However, there are times when changing the octave moves the melody too far up or down for an individual's range. In this situation, finding a new key in between the two octaves is usually the solution. Changing the key of a piece of music is called **transposing** or **transposition**. This subject is dealt with in lesson 9.

# LESSON SEVEN

## The Tie

A **tie** is a curved line which connects two notes with the **same** position on the staff. The tie tells you to sing the **first** note only, and to hold it for the length of both notes. In the following example, the note G should be held for **six** beats.

There are two common reasons for using ties. One is that this is the only way of indicating that a note is to be held across a bar line (as shown above) and the other is that a tie is a way of increasing the length of a note within a bar. If you look at the written music for the song "Scarborough Fair", you will notice ties used both of these ways. In bar 2 there is an eighth note tied to a quarter note and there are several instances of ties used to indicate notes held across the bar line. Here is another example to help you become more familiar with the use of ties. Once again, try clapping the rhythms while counting the beats out loud. Then try singing the rhythms while tapping your foot on the beat. Make sure you don't start tapping your foot on the written rhythms instead of evenly on each beat.

# Syncopation

When you count along with music, there is often a natural pattern of accents on each beat. However, when ties are used with eighth notes, this often displaces some of the natural accents from on the beat to off the beat (in between the beats). This effect is known as syncopation. The preceding example contains several syncopated rhythms created by the use of ties. Here is another example of syncopation. Listen to the way the accent is thrown to the **+** (**and**) part of the count by the use of ties.

# The Eighth Rest

This is an **eighth rest**.
It indicates **half a beat of silence**.

 **46**

There are two common positions for eighth note rests – off the beat and on the beat. These are demonstrated in the following example which is sung with the syllable **ba**.

**47**

The use of eighth rests on the beat is a common way of achieving syncopated rhythms. Here is an example to help you understand the use of eighth rests. This example is written in the style of Bobby McFerrin, who often mimics instrumental solos with his voice. This style developed out of Jazz "scat" singing, a technique using wordless vocal lines which are often improvised. The progression used for this example is the **12 Bar Blues**. This progression is the basis of thousands of popular songs. This example is sung using the syllable **ba**. Try some other syllables with this melody as well.

# 48  Jamaica Farewell

This traditional Caribbean song makes much use of syncopated rhythms. It is written here in the key of D major, which was comfortable for both our female and male vocalists. The difference is that they are singing it in different octaves. You will also notice slight differences in timing and phrasing between the two versions. This is a natural part of each singer's personal expression. Phrasing, interpretation and improvisation are dealt with in lesson 8.  Once you have learned the song, you could try singing it in several other keys until you find the most comfortable key for your voice. The key note (**do**) in this case is the final note of the song (a **D** note). To sing this in another key (e.g. key of F) play and sustain an **F** note on a keyboard or guitar while you sing the final phrase of the song. Check to see that your voice is finishing on the note F along with the instrument. Then sing the whole song in that key. Try keys which are both higher and lower than D by a small distance at first. Eventually it is a good idea to try every song you know in all possible keys until you find the most comfortable key for your voice for each song. Then you can instantly tell the musicians who accompany you which key you prefer to sing the song in. This will always be appreciated and can save a lot of time at rehearsals.

2. Sounds of laughter everywhere,
   And the dancing girls sway, to and fro,
   I must declare my heart is there,
   Though I've been from Maine to Mexico, but I',m
   Sad to say, I'm on my way, etc.

3. Down at the markets, you can hear,
   Ladies cry out, while on their heads they bear,
   Ackie rice, salt fish are nice,
   And the rum is fine any time of year, but I'm
   Sad to say, I'm on my way, etc.

# The Lead-in

Sometimes a song does not begin on the first beat of a bar. Any notes which come before the first full bar are called **lead-in notes** (or "pick-up notes", or an "anacrusis"). When lead-in notes are used, the last bar is also incomplete. The notes in the lead-in and the notes in the last bar add up to one full bar. The song **Greensleeves** on the following page contains one lead-in note. When lead-in notes are used, it means that the melody begins before the accompaniment. This means you will probably need a reference pitch for your starting note in order to be sure you are singing the correct pitch. Before you begin the song, get somebody to play first the note or chord of the key, and then the starting note on an instrument. Hum the starting note to yourself for a few seconds until you are confident of the note and then begin counting the song in. An example of this is shown below for the song **Greensleeves**. The chord is an **E minor** chord because the song has been recorded in the key of E minor and the lead-in note is also an **E** note.

49

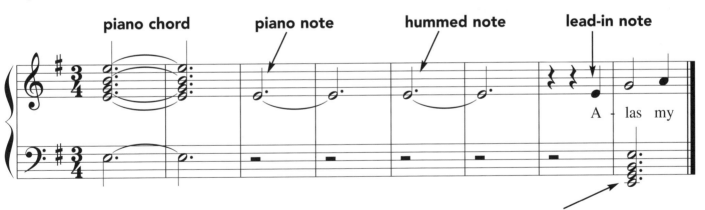

**Accompaniment begins in first full bar**

# First and Second Endings

The next song contains **first and second endings**. The **first** time you sing through the verse, sing the **first ending** ( 1. ), then go back to the beginning. The **second** time you sing through the verse, sing the **second ending** ( 2. ) instead of the first.

# 50. Greensleeves

This traditional English folk song is written here in the key of **E minor**, which is the relative minor of G major. It is in ¾ time and once again begins with a lead-in note. Notice the **F♯** note written as a key signature for the key of E minor in this song, reminding you to treat all F notes as F♯. Notice also the frequent use of other sharps in this song. When sharps or flats occur that are not part of the key signature, they are called **accidentals**. An accidental is a temporary alteration to the pitch of a note and is cancelled by a bar line. Both our male vocalist and our female vocalist found E minor a comfortable key for singing this song. Once again, the difference is that they are singing the same notes in different octaves.

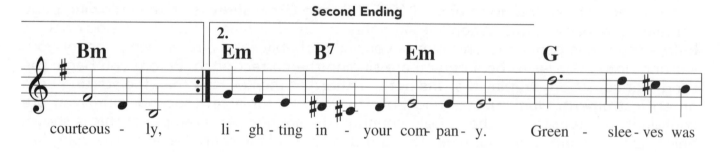

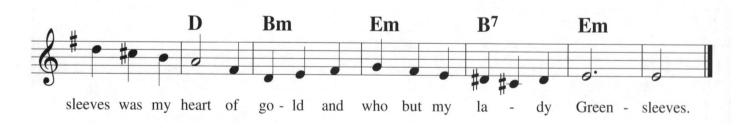

2. I have been ready at your hand
   To grant whatever you would crave,
   I have both wagered life and land,
   Your love and good will for to have.

3. I bought thee petticoats of the best,
   The cloth so fine as it might be,
   I gave thee jewels for the chest,
   And all this cost I spent on thee.

4. Well, I will pray to God on high,
   That thou my constancy may'st see,
   For I am still thy lover true;
   Come once again and love me.

# LESSON EIGHT

## The Triplet

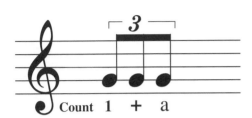

Count 1 + a

A **triplet** is a group of **three** evenly spaced notes played within one beat. Eighth note triplets are indicated by three eighth notes grouped together by a bracket (or a curved line) and the numeral **3**. The eighth note triplets are sung with one third of a beat each. Triplets are easy to understand once you have heard them played. Listen to example 51 on the CD to hear the effect of triplets.

 ### 51  How to Count Triplets

| Written | 1 | + | a | 2 | + | a | 3 | + | a | 4 | + | a |
| Say | 1 | and | ah | 2 | and | ah | 3 | and | ah | 4 | and | ah |

 ### 52  Amazing Grace

This traditional Gospel song makes use of triplets in bars 1, 5, 9 and 13. It is in ¾ time and also contains a lead-in.

# *Swing Rhythms*

A **swing rhythm** can be created by playing or singing only the first and third notes of a triplet. There are several different ways of writing swing rhythms. To understand them it is worth using one musical example written in various ways. First, using the syllable **ba** sing example 53 which contains eighth note triplets.

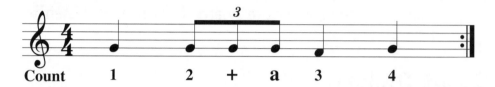

This variation has the first and second notes of the triplet group tied. This gives the example a swing feel.

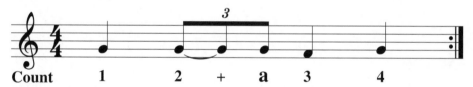

The two eighth note triplets tied together in example 54 can be replaced by a quarter note.

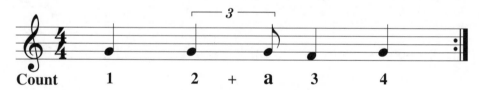

To simplify notation, it is common to replace the  and to write at the start of the piece as illustrated below in example 56.

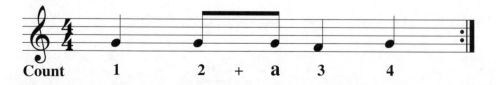

The previous three examples sound exactly the same. They are just different ways of notating the same melody.

## 57.0    St James Infirmary

This song was made famous by Louis Armstrong. It is played and sung with a swing feel. This means that all the eighth notes in the song are swung. There are many songs in various styles that have a swing feel. They are particularly common in Blues and Jazz as well as Gospel, Rock and Country music.

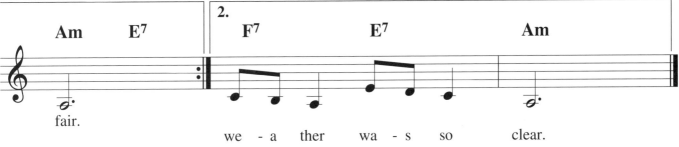

## 57.1    St James Infirmary Version 2

The second version of this song on the recording is in the key of E minor. Once again, there are slight differences in phrasing between the two versions. Sing along with the version that feels most comfortable for your vocal range.

# Interpretation and Improvisation

Every singer has his or her own way of interpreting a song. It is rare that two singers will sing a song exactly the same way. Often a singer will learn a new song by getting the basic melody from another vocalist's version and then changing it to suit their own style. This may mean varying the lengths of notes, changing the rhythms, changing a few notes to different pitches, or even totally changing the melody. As long as the new melody fits with the lyrics, this is perfectly OK. In fact, some of the greatest recordings of songs have come about by the vocalist completely changing the melody and the accompanying musicians fitting their parts to the new version of the melody. Another situation where experience at improvising comes in handy is in writing songs. Many times you or a friend may have some lyrics and you need to put a melody to them. There is always more than one way of doing this. Written below are two different ways of approaching a simple lyric. One is in $\frac{3}{4}$ time in a major key and the other is in $\frac{4}{4}$ time and in a minor key.

 **58**

In most melodies there is a natural accent on the first beat of the bar. This can be used to stress particular words in a song. In the first phrase of this example, the emphasis is on the word "woke" rather than the first word "I" at the beginning of the phrase because there is a lead-in note. In the second phrase, "I" is emphasised because it falls on the first beat of the bar.

 **59**

In this example, the first accent falls on the word "early" because there is a three note lead-in. In the second phrase, the word "early" is once again emphasised but a higher note is used the second time to add variety. Notice also that the word "morning" has been changed to mornin' in this version. This type of alteration is common in many styles of music. It really depends on what is most appropriate for the style. For example, perfectly correct grammar can often sound out of place in a Rock or Blues song, as songs in these styles are based on a language tradition which has always included slang.

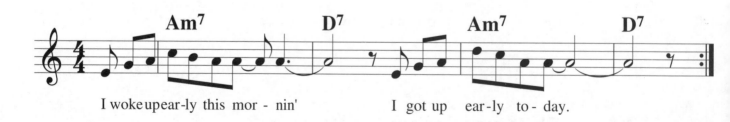

As you can hear, these two approaches to the same lyric are quite different. The meaning of the lyrics, along with the style of music you are singing, as well as the instrumental combination you are fitting in with will often determine the way you approach a melody. Try experimenting with different approaches to melodies you already know as well as creating your own new melodies.

# Sixteenth Notes

 This is a **sixteenth note**.
It lasts for **one quarter** of a beat.
There are **four** sixteenth notes in one beat.
There are **16** sixteenth notes in one bar
of 4/4 time.

Four sixteenth notes joined together.

Count: 1  e  +  a

Say:  one 'ee' and 'ah'

##  60  How to Count Sixteenth Notes

Tap your foot on each beat to help you keep time as you sing this example.

Count  1 e + a 2 e + a 3 e + a 4 e + a

##  61

Often in songs you will find two sixteenth notes grouped together with an eighth note as demonstrated in this example.

Count  1 e + 2 e + 3 + a 4 +   1 e + 2 + a 3 + 4 +

##  62

Now try this example which combines sixteenth notes with some of the other note values you have learnt. Another figure used here is the dotted eighth note and sixteenth note grouping. The dotted eighth note lasts for three quarters of a beat and the sixteenth note makes up the last part of the beat. Once you understand sixteenth notes, you have covered all of the common note types and basic rhythms used in song melodies.

Count  1 e + a 2 + 3 + 4 e + a  1 e + a 2 + 3 + 4+

1 + a 2 e + a 3 e + 4 +   1  2 + 3 + 4

**63   Swing Low, Sweet Chariot**

The first version of this song is in the key of E, as shown by the key signature (four sharps). The second half of the melody contains several examples of improvisation. If you have trouble with any of the timing in the song, practice the rhythm figures on one note as in the earlier rhythm examples. Also try singing along with the recording and try to feel the timing and then imitate it.

2. If you get there before I do,
   Coming for to carry me home,
   Tell all my friends I'm coming too,
   Coming for to carry me home.

3. The brightest day that ever I saw,
   Coming for to carry me home,
   When Jesus wash'd my sins away,
   Coming for to carry me home.

**64 Swing Low, Sweet Chariot Version 2**

The second version of this song is in the key of G as shown below. This version also contains improvised phrases in the second half. As with previous songs, sing along with the version which best suits your particular vocal range.

# LESSON NINE

# Transposing

You will notice that when there are two versions of songs in this book they are often in different keys. This is because everyone's voice range is different and while one key is perfect for one singer, the same key will be uncomfortable (too high or too low) for another. Often when you learn a new song, you will find that it in contains notes that are either too high or too low for your voice. The solution is to experiment with singing the melody either lower or higher until you find a comfortable range for your voice. When you do this, you are actually changing the key of the melody. This is called **transposing**. The ability to transpose is an important skill for a singer to develop. When you get together with another musician, you may find that you both know the same song but you have to determine the key which is most comfortable for you to sing in. If you know how to transpose and can say "I sing this one in D" (or G, or B flat, or any other key) you can save a lot of time which might otherwise be wasted stumbling around ignorantly until you find a key and even then don't know what "key" means, which means you have to go through the same process again next time. The easiest way to transpose written music is to write the **scale degrees** (**do = 1**, **re = 2**, **mi = 3**, etc) under the original melody and then work out which notes correspond to those scale degrees in the key you want to transpose to. To transpose by ear, you will need to relate your pitches to an instrument to know what key you are transposing to. The examples below demonstrate the first part of the melody of **"Swing Low, Sweet Chariot"** transposed from the key of **G** to the keys of **D** and **F**. Try this technique with some of the other songs in the book, or any other songs you know.

## Key of G Major

## Key of D Major

## Key of F Major

# The Six Eight Time Signature

This is the **six eight** time signature.
There are six eighth notes in one bar of $\frac{6}{8}$ time. The six eighth notes are divided into two groups of three.

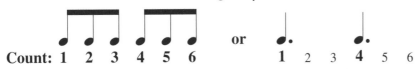

When playing or singing $\frac{6}{8}$ time there are **two** beats within each bar with each beat being a **dotted quarter note**. (This is different to $\frac{4}{4}$ and $\frac{3}{4}$ time where each beat is a quarter note). Another useful time signature based on eighth notes is twelve eight ($\frac{12}{8}$) which means there are twelve eighth notes per bar. Many Blues songs are written in $\frac{12}{8}$ time.

 **65 House of the Rising Sun**

This traditional American song is in $\frac{6}{8}$ time and is written here in the **key of E minor**.

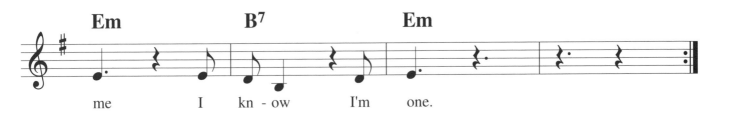

54

 **66. House of the Rising Sun Version 2**

The second recorded version of this song is in the key of **B♭** minor, which means it has been transposed up an interval of a diminished 5th from the key of E minor. As mentioned earlier, an interval is a measurement of distance in music. A knowledge of intervals is particularly useful for transposing, as well as helping you to learn songs more quickly by sight or by ear. Ask your teacher to show you how intervals work by demonstrating them on the keyboard.

2. My mother she's a tailor
   She sews those new blue jeans
   My husband he's a gamblin' man,
   Drinks down in New Orleans.

3. My husband he's a gambler,
   He goes from town to town
   And the only time he's satisfied
   Is when he drinks his liquor down.

4. Now, the only thing that a gambler needs
   Is a suitcase and a trunk
   And the only time he's ever satisfied
   Is when he's on a drunk.

5. He fills his glasses up to the brim
   And he passes the cards around
   And the only pleasure he gets out of life
   Is ramblin' from town to town.

6. Go tell my baby sister
   Not to do what I have done
   Shun that house in New Orleans
   They call the risin' sun.

7. If I had listened to what my mother said
   I'd have been at home today
   But I was so young and foolish
   I let a rambler lead me astray.

8. Well it's a-one foot on the platform
   And the other foot on the train
   I'm goin back to New Orleans
   To wear that ball and chain.

9. I'm goin back to New Orleans
   My race is nearly run.
   I'm goin back to end my life
   In the house of the risin sun.

# Harmony and Chords

Harmony can be thought of as the notes that support and add character to a melody. The basic building blocks of harmony are chords. A chord is a group of notes played simultaneously (e.g. strumming on a guitar). Like scales, there are many different types of chords, the most common being the **major chord**. All major chords contain three notes, taken from the major scale of the same letter name. These three notes are the 1 (first), 3 (third) and 5 (fifth) notes of the major scale, so the **chord formula** for the major chord is: **1 3 5**. If these notes were taken from the C major scale the chord would be a **C major chord**, usually just called a **C chord**. Chords are represented by symbols usually written above the vocal melody on sheet music. The symbol for a C chord is the letter **C**, as shown below. The symbol for a D (major) chord is the letter **D**. The symbol for an E flat chord would be **E♭**

*Chord Symbol*

## The C Major Chord

*Notes in Chord*

| C | E | G |
|---|---|---|
| 1 | 3 | 5 |

The C major chord is constructed from the C major scale. Using the above chord formula on the C major scale below, it can be seen that the C major chord contains the notes C, E and G.

## C Major Scale

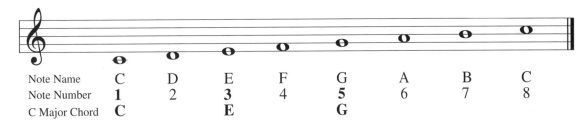

| Note Name | C | D | E | F | G | A | B | C |
|---|---|---|---|---|---|---|---|---|
| Note Number | 1 | 2 | 3 | 4 | 5 | 6 | 7 | 8 |
| C Major Chord | C | | E | | G | | | |

The example below demonstrates a short melody in ⁴⁄₄ time in the key of G accompanied by three major chords – G, C and D. The chord symbols for these chords are written above the melody. Notice also the key signature and the time signature at the start of the music. Listen to the example on the CD to hear the effect created by the combination of melody and chords.

 **67**

# How Chords Relate to Scales

Just as a chord can be built on the first note of a scale, it is possible to build chords on all the other notes of the scale. To build a chord on any note, you simply use that note to name the chord (e.g. **D**), and then add the note two letter names further up the scale (**F**) and then add the note two letter names above that (**A**). This would give you a chord containing the notes D, F and A. The first note is called the root of the chord (D), the middle note is called the third (F) and the last note is called the fifth (A). Because of the uneven pattern of tones and semitones in the major scale, not all of these notes are the same distance apart. For this reason, when you build chords on all the notes of the major scale, you end up with different types of chords. E.g. the chord built on the first note of the C major scale is a C major chord, but the chord built on the second note is a **D minor chord**. If you are interested in learning more about how chords are made from scales it is worth taking a few lessons from a good music teacher. Ask your local music store to recommend someone.

As you can see, just as there are major and minor scales, there are also major and minor chords. There are also many other types of chords all of which have different names and sounds. Each type has a different combination of notes and a specific chord formula. If you look at most sheet music you will see chord symbols written above the melody, symbols such as **C**, **Am**, **B♭7**, **E7♯9**, etc. All these symbols describe chords which have different types of sounds. The reason a certain set of chords works well with a particular melody is that both the melody and the chords are made up of notes from the same key. When putting a melody and chords together, the basic principle is that at the beginning of each bar or where there is a long sustained note, or any time there is a new chord, one of the notes of the chord played at that point should be the same note that is used in the melody at that point. E.g. if the melody has a G long note at the beginning of a bar, any chord used at that point should contain a G note. This doesn't mean it has to be a G chord, it could be any chord which has G as one of its notes. E.g. a C chord or an E minor chord or an A7 chord all contain the note G. Understanding chords can be quite difficult at first and is a lot easier if you relate it to an instrument capable of playing chords (e.g. guitar or keyboard). To learn the basics of these instruments, see *10 Easy Lessons for Guitar*, or *10 Easy Lessons for Piano*. Both of these books contain many of the songs used in this book, so you can directly apply the new knowledge about chords to songs you already know.

# Arpeggios

An **arpeggio** is a chord which is played or sung one note at a time. As it is not possible to sing two notes simultaneously with one voice, singing an arpeggio is the only way a singer can sing a chord. The example below shows the arpeggios of **C**, **F** and **G** major sung with the syllable **la**. It is also possible to sing arpeggios of any other type of chord, e.g. minor arpeggios, seventh arpeggios, diminished arpeggios, etc. Arpeggios are often used in song melodies. The reason they work so well is that they fit perfectly with any accompanying chord because both the melody and chords contain exactly the same notes.

 **68**

# Chord Progressions

Chords are usually played in a repeating sequence called a **chord progression**. A chord progression may repeat every 2, 4, 8, 12 or 16 bars. This could mean that the progression is repeated many times within a verse (as in many Rock songs), or that the chord progression may be the same length as the verse. Once again, the best way to learn about chords and chord progressions is to learn a bit of basic guitar or keyboard. Many singers like to accompany themselves on guitar or keyboard, so some knowledge in this area can have a practical value as well as helping you learn more about music. On the recording of the songs in the book, the vocalist sings the melody and is accompanied by chords played by guitar and/or keyboard. The bass plays a line which is made up of notes from the particular key the song is in and helps to outline the chords with these notes. The drums lay down the rhythm as well as adding drive and drama to the songs. Drum parts are made up of notes of various values (quarter notes, eighth notes, triplets, etc). Put all these parts together and you have the three basic elements of music – **melody**, **harmony** and **rhythm**.

# LESSON TEN

# Performing in Public

Performing in public can be both exciting and frightening for any new performer whether they are a singer, an instrumentalist, an actor or simply someone giving a speech on a social occasion. Many people who are shy at first develop into dynamic performers who can both entertain and captivate an audience. Like any other skill, performing in public takes time to develop and there is much to be learned from watching other performers. To begin with, the best approach can be to simply take a deep breath, walk on, smile, look the audience in the eye and begin with a song you are very familiar with. If you are nervous, concentrate on the sound you and your accompanist(s) are making and move your body to the music in any way that feels good. If you are able to enjoy yourself, this will communicate itself to the audience. Nervousness can be turned into excitement and positive energy and can actually make your natural reactions and responses to the music quicker.

# Overcoming Nerves

There are three essential elements in overcoming nervousness and turning it into a positive. The first of these is **knowing your material well**. This means thoroughly rehearsing all aspects of each song before you even consider performing them. If you are unsure of the words, or the notes or timing of either the melody or the accompaniment, it is not surprising that you would become nervous. The more certain you are of these things, the more you are free concentrate on expressing the meaning of the lyrics and making great music.

The second element is **being comfortable with your equipment and your environment**. Most public performances involve the use of microphones. Using a microphone will be discussed later in this lesson. When you are on stage, it is important to be comfortable using the microphone and to not be startled by hearing yourself through the PA system or foldback speakers. If possible, it is advisable to have a sound check before members of the public arrive. Most professional ensembles have a thorough sound check in which all the equipment is tested individually and together at least an hour (preferably more) before the show. This allows everybody to become comfortable with the sound of the room as well as the equipment. If you learn a bit about PA systems you can also communicate your requirements and preferences to the person operating the sound system.

The third element is **trusting yourself**. If you are considering singing in public, you are probably fairly confident that you are making a good sound when you sing and you have probably received compliments from friends as well. In this case, you should be able to sing equally well or better in public, particularly once an audience begins to respond. Your body instinctively knows every aspect of producing a good vocal sound, so it is usually just a case of "letting go" and becoming part of the music. The more you can become the character in each song (like an actor) the more convincing your performance will be and the better you will be able to deliver it.

# Eye Contact

When you sing, you are telling a story to the audience. Look at them as you tell this story and they will respond. Obviously you cannot look at everybody, but you can pick out certain people (e.g. someone wearing bright clothing or someone with a bald spot on their head). Another option is to look towards the people in the middle of the audience. Change your focus from time to time to include all sections of the audience. Everybody will feel you are communicating with them personally and will enjoy your performance more. Remember that when people go to hear a public performance, they are looking forward to having a good time. This means they are automatically prepared to like you even before they see or hear you, so in reality the performance should be a positive experience for everyone involved. Another important aspect of any performance is eye contact between the performers. The fact that an ensemble are communicating well and obviously enjoying themselves makes the audience feel good too.

# Stage Presence and Stage Craft

Most great performers have what is commonly known as good **stage presence**. Stage presence is the total impression created in the minds and emotions of the audience by the performer(s). This impression is made up of both the drama of the music and speech and the drama of the visual performance. As mentioned earlier, there is much to be learned by watching other performers. It is essential for aspiring performers to see professional singers, musicians, actors or other entertainers perform live as often as possible in the early stages. You can do this by going to shows or by watching performances on video or television. Notice how each performer communicates with both their ensemble and the audience. Learn how they use both spontaneous and choreographed movement. Watch how the music is expressed through their bodies and facial expressions as well as their sound. Notice whether they use humour or not, or any other element of public performance you can think of. All these things can be learned and developed and can be described as the various parts of stage craft.

# Developing Your Own Style

Many performers learn their stage craft and their ability to express their vocal or instrumental technique by copying other performers at first and then ultimately adapting what they have learned to form their own unique style and presence. Ray Charles seriously studied Nat King Cole's style of singing and playing early in his career, but later developed his own intensely personal style which has little in common with Nat King Cole. This is similar to the way students of visual art are taught to copy the works of masters early in their development. By doing this, the student learns about color, form, design, balance, etc. as well as learning technique. However, this is only the first step in the process. The idea is to master the practical elements in order to be able to go on and express your own feelings, ideas and personality through your own work. Copying a Rembrandt or Picasso painting is an extremely valuable exercise for an art student, but it is not an end in itself. So it is with singing and performing. Learn all you can from performers you admire, whether it is their vocal technique, their musicianship or their stagecraft. Study them in detail and work diligently on everything you learn, particularly in the early stages of your development. However, it is not recommended that you slavishly copy any particular person's style over a long period of time (unless you want to be a comedy act). As your confidence develops along with your personal feelings for the music you are performing, your own style will begin to emerge by itself if you let it. As you practice and perform, notice the things that you feel most intensely about. These are the seeds which will grow into your own vital style if you are true to them and develop them properly.

# Microphones

It is essential for all singers to know how to use a microphone. Even if you mainly sing in a choir or in small rooms with only a piano accompaniment, it is likely that you will be required to use a microphone at some stage. If you sing with a band, you will use a microphone every time you perform. It is a good idea to have your own microphone that you are comfortable with, even if the venue you are performing at provides them along with the PA system.

## Microphones for Performing Live

There are several different types of microphones available. Each of them is best suited to a different musical situation (e.g. live band performance, or recording session).
The type of microphone most commonly used for live performances is the **dynamic microphone**. These microphones contain a diaphragm and a coil which is activated when the voice causes it to vibrate. Dynamic microphones are normally uni-directional, or "front sensitive" which means that sounds entering from the sides of the microphone are amplified less than sound entering from the top or front. Because of their resistance to feedback (the piercing sound made when a microphone picks up the sound coming from the speakers and amplifies it again) uni-directional microphones are particularly useful in a live band environment.

Microphones which are omni-directional receive sound equally from all sides of the microphone. This makes them useful for back-up vocals in situations where two or more singers share one microphone but they are not recommended for a lead singer in a live band situation.

Before you buy a microphone it is advisable to visit a music store and try out some in the store. The Shure SM58 microphone shown in the photo below is a typical professional quality uni-directional dynamic microphone and is one of the most common microphones used by bands. There are also other good microphones available which are of a similar design. If you intend to perform in public regularly, it is worth spending a little extra on a good microphone as it will make you sound better and make you more comfortable with your sound on stage.

**Shure SM58 - A Typical Dynamic Microphone**

# Microphone Technique

When using a uni-directional microphone, there are some important fundamentals to learn, as detailed below.

• Hold the microphone in the palm of your hand with your fingers curled loosely around it, just tightly enough to avoid dropping the microphone but not tightly enough to cause tension.

• Sing directly into the microphone. Many beginning performers unintentionally move sideways away from the mic as they are singing. This means that the sound is lost to the audience and they can't understand what is being sung. Practice moving around and singing into the microphone. Make sure that when you move sideways your hand keeps the mic in relatively the same position so that your voice goes directly into it at all times. The best position for the mic is just below your mouth at about a 45 degree angle so that the centre of the head of the mic is aimed directly at your mouth.

• Depending on the natural volume of your voice along with the sensitivity of the equipment being used, the distance between your mouth and the microphone should vary between one and ten centimetres. During loud passages the microphone should be pulled back slightly in order to balance the overall volume. This will also reduce the chances of "PEE POP", which is the term used to describe the effect created by "hard" consonants such as **b, d, g** and particularly **p** exploding out of the singer's mouth and onto the microphone (this can be overcome by articulating consonants lightly, along with moving the microphone slightly away from the mouth when accenting words or sounds).

• Avoid touching the microphone with your mouth, as the sound will distort and unwanted sounds produced by the contact will be amplified along with your singing.

• If you are moving around while you are singing, stay away from the "front of house" speakers or you may experience feedback problems. As long as you are somewhere behind or at the most, level with the front of house speakers, but a reasonable distance from them, you shouldn't have any feedback problems.

# Studio Microphones

In a recording studio, a different type of microphone called a **condenser microphone** is often used. These microphones are much more sensitive than dynamic microphones. Since the singer in the studio is usually hearing the accompaniment through headphones, the microphone can afford to be more sensitive at a much lower volume. Condenser mics pick up many more subtleties and provide a deeper and more detailed sound than dynamic mics. Condenser mics also contain a capacitor and need electric power to run. When singing into a condenser mic, you can afford to be a little further back from it. However, there is generally a best position or "sweet spot" where your voice will sound best. This varies from one voice to another and from one condenser microphone to another, so when you are in a recording situation and are unsure of the sound, it is best to try a few different mics and experiment with the positioning of each one before deciding what sounds best. The recording engineer will usually be able to hear your voice and choose a microphone which will complement it.

# Warming Up

Before you begin a performance, it is a good idea to go through some kind of warm up routine. This will help loosen your muscles and help you relax, as well as getting your blood flowing and helping to focus your mind for the performance. The first steps in any warm up routine are usually breathing and stretching exercises. Start with the breathing exercise explained in lesson 1. Then do some gentle movements and gradually stretch more as your body begins to feel more flexible. The next step is to sing some sustained notes using an open vowel sound such as **ah**. Gradually move your voice around higher and lower pitches and then sing a couple of scales. The exercise for moving between registers (sliding between octaves) on page 32 is particularly useful. Next try some exercises using various vowel sounds, such as the one given on page 29. The final stage is to sing a verse from the song you intend to begin the performance with. Include any physical movements you normally use when performing the song. This should get you in the mood for the performance and make you keen to get out there and begin.

# Looking After Your Voice

Like anyone involved in regular physical activity, it is important for a singer to keep fit. All the muscles, ligaments, tendons, etc. used in singing and stage movement require regular exercise to keep them flexible and in the best condition for performing. It is also important not to strain your voice, as this can lead to poor technique along with a lessening of the sound quality of your voice. In extreme cases such as repeated shouting, this can lead to vocal nodules. These are growths on the vocal cords which can cause permanent damage.

Nodules usually occur in Rock singers who sing with a rough technique at high volume (shouting) over extended periods, often in an attempt to compete with the volume of electric guitars played through large amplifiers. If you are singing with a band, it is essential to have adequate foldback. Foldback speakers are ones which are aimed at the performers rather than the audience. They are there so the performers can hear themselves properly when amplified through a PA system. If you are having trouble hearing yourself, you should never sing louder to try to overcome the situation. Instead, you will either need to turn the foldback up or get the instrumentalists to turn their amplifiers down, or both. Many beginning electric guitarists and drummers are not used to playing at quieter volumes, but it is essential that they learn. Otherwise you may end up with vocal damage.

When rehearsing songs, don't forget that dynamics are an essential part of music. If you always play and sing too loud, you have nowhere to go. Get the musicians accompanying you to play at a comfortable "middle" volume and work out the best places in the song to increase or decrease the volume for dramatic effect. When performing, everything you do either as a singer or an ensemble should have the sole purpose of communicating the song to the audience. This means moving them emotionally rather than deafening them.

Another aspect of looking after your voice is drinking plenty of water. Other liquids can adversely affect the sound of your voice, but water keeps the throat and larynx lubricated without affecting the sound. It also has the added bonus of preventing dehydration if you are using a lot of energy on stage. As well as this, a sensible diet and regular exercise will help keep your body in the best possible condition for singing and performing.

# Approach to Practice

Regardless of the style of music you sing, It is important to have a correct approach to practice. You will benefit more from several short practices (e.g. 20-30 minutes per day) than one or two long sessions per week. This is especially so in the early stages, because your muscles and your voice are still developing. If you want to become a great singer you will obviously have to practice more as time goes on, but it is still better to work on new things a bit at a time. Get one small piece of information and learn it well before going on to the next topic. Make sure each new thing you learn is thoroughly worked into your singing. This way you won't forget it, and you can build on everything you learn.

In a practice session you should divide your time evenly between the study of new material and the revision of past work. It is a common mistake for semi-advanced students to practice only the songs they can already sing well. Although this is enjoyable, it is not a satisfactory method of practice. You should also try to correct mistakes and experiment with new ideas. It is the author's belief that the guidance of an experienced teacher will be an invaluable aid in your progress. To develop good timing, it is essential that you always practice with a metronome (or drum machine). Beginning singers are often particularly weak in this area. As mentioned earlier, your timing and all-round musicianship will improve dramatically if you learn to accompany yourself on keyboard or guitar.

Apart from practicing your actual singing technique, it is important to spend time thinking about the lyrics to each song and how you can bring meaning to the song with your interpretation. From this point of view it is useful to learn a bit about acting. Maybe you could talk to an actor or take a few drama lessons. It is also useful to look at film scripts and notice the director's remarks and directions which are often written in.

# Listening

Apart from books and sheet music, your most important source of information will be recordings. Listen to albums which feature great singers. Regardless of the style of music you prefer to sing, it is important to listen to many different styles, in order to hear the widest possible variety of interpretations and expressions. There is something to be learned from every style of music and singing. It is a useful exercise to listen to several different recordings of the same song performed by different singers. Listen to their phrasing, their timing, their note choices, the tempo they choose, and the style of accompaniment. By doing this with several songs, you will soon work out your own preferences as well as getting valuable ideas for how to approach other songs and how to write your own arrangements. When you are listening to albums, sing along with the songs and try to copy the sounds you are hearing. This helps you absorb the music and before long, it will start to come out in your own style. It is also valuable to sing along with albums sometimes imitating what you are hearing and sometimes improvising. This is good ear training and is also a lot of fun.

For more books and recordings by the author, visit: **www.bentnotes.com**

# Recording Yourself

From time to time it is a good idea to record your performances or practice sessions. Unless you have studio quality equipment, the tone quality you hear on the recording may not be completely accurate, but any recording will pick up timing and relative pitch accurately. As you listen back to yourself, pay particular attention to areas you think are particularly weak or particularly strong. Anything you think sounds good is worth developing further and anything that doesn't (e.g. timing, or pitching on high notes) should be the focus of your practice sessions until it is turned into a strength.

# Glossary of Musical Terms

**Accidental** — a sign used to show a temporary change in pitch of a note (i.e. sharp ♯, flat ♭, double sharp 𝄪, double flat ♭♭, or natural ♮). The sharps or flats in a key signature are not regarded as accidentals.

**Ad lib** — to be played at the performer's own discretion.

**Allegretto** — moderately fast.

**Allegro** — fast and lively.

**Andante** — an easy walking pace.

**Arpeggio** — the playing of a chord in single note fashion.

**Bar** — a division of music occurring between two bar lines (also called a 'measure').

**Bar chord** — a chord played with one finger lying across all six strings on the guitar.

**Bar line** — a vertical line drawn across the staff dividing the music into equal sections called bars.

**Bass** — the lower regions of pitch in general. On guitar, the 4th, 5th and 6th strings.

**Chord** — a combination of three or more different notes played together.

**Chord progression** — a series of chords played as a musical unit (e.g. as in a song).

**Clef** — a sign placed at the beginning of each staff of music which fixes the location of a particular note on the staff, and hence the location of all other notes.

**Coda** — an ending section of music, signified by the sign ⊕ .

**Common time** — and indication of $\frac{4}{4}$ time — four quarter note beats per bar (also indicated by **C** ).

**D.C al fine** — a repeat from the sign (indicated thus 𝄋 ) to the word 'fine'.

**Dynamics** — the varying degrees of softness (indicated by the term 'piano') and loudness (indicated by the term 'forte') in music.

**Eighth note** — a note with the value of half a beat in $\frac{4}{4}$ time, indicated thus ♪ (also called a quaver).

**The eighth note rest** — indicating half a beat of silence is written: ♪

**Enharmonic** — describes the difference in notation, but not in pitch, of two notes.

**Fermata** — a sign, ⌢ , used to indicate that a note or chord is held to the player's own discretion (also called a 'pause sign').

**Flat** — a sign, (♭)used to lower the pitch of a note by one semitone.

**Forte** — loud. Indicated by the sign 𝑓 .

**Half note** — a note with the value of two beats in $\frac{4}{4}$ time, indicated thus: 𝅗𝅥 (also called a minim). The half note rest, indicating two beats of silence, is written: ▬ on the third staff line.

**Harmony** — the simultaneous sounding of two or more different notes.

**Interval** — the distance between any two notes of different pitches.

**Key** — describes the notes used in a composition in regards to the major or minor scale from which they are taken; e.g. a piece 'in the key of C major' describes the melody, chords, etc., as predominantly consisting of the notes, **C, D, E, F, G, A,** and **B** — i.e. from the **C** scale.

**Key signature** — a sign, placed at the beginning of each stave of music, directly after the clef, to indicate the key of a piece. The sign consists of a certain number of sharps or flats, which represent the sharps or flats found in the scale of the piece's key.

**Leger lines** — small horizontal lines upon which notes are written when their pitch is either above or below the range of the staff.

**Legato** — smoothly, well connected.

**Major scale** — a series of eight notes in alphabetical order based on the interval sequence tone - tone - semitone - tone - tone - tone - semitone, giving the familiar sound **do re mi fa so la ti do**.

**Melody** — a group of notes of varying pitch and duration, and having a recognizable musical shape.

**Metronome** — a device which indicates the number of beats per minute, and which can be adjusted in accordance to the desired tempo.

**Moderato** — at a moderate pace.**Natural** — a sign (♮)used to cancel out the effect of a sharp or flat. The word is also used to describe the notes **A, B, C, D, E, F** and **G**; e.g. 'the natural notes'.

**Note** — a single sound with a given pitch and duration.

**Octave** — the distance between any given note with a set frequency, and another note with exactly double that frequency. Both notes will have the same letter name.

**Open voicing** — a chord that has the notes spread out between both hands on the keyboard.

**Pitch** — the sound produced by a note, determined by the frequency of the string vibrations. The pitch relates to a note being referred to as 'high' or 'low'.

**Plectrum** — a small object (often of a triangular shape) made of plastic which is used to pick or strum the strings of a guitar.

**Position** — a term used to describe the location of the left hand on the guitar fret board. The left hand position is determined by the fret location of the first finger. The 1st position refers to the 1st to 4th frets. The 3rd position refers to the 3rd to 6th frets and so on.

**Quarter note** — a note with the value of one beat in $\frac{4}{4}$ time, indicated thus ♩ (also called a crotchet). The quarter note rest, indicating one beat of silence, is written: 𝄽 .

**Repeat signs** — used to indicate a repeat of a section of music, by means of two dots placed before a double bar line.

**Rhythm** — the note after which a chord or scale is named (also called 'key note').

**Semitone** — the smallest interval used in conventional music. On guitar, it is a distance of one fret.

**Sharp** — a sign ( ♯ ) used to raise the pitch of a note by one semitone.

**Staccato** — to play short and detached. Indicated by a dot placed above the note.

**Staff** — five parallel lines together with four spaces, upon which music is written.

**Syncopation** — the placing of an accent on a normally unaccented beat.

**Tempo** — the speed of a piece.

**Tie** — a curved line joining two or more notes of the same pitch, where the second note(s) is not played, but its time value is added to that of the first note.

**Timbre** — a quality which distinguishes a note produced on one instrument from the same note produced on any other instrument (also called 'tone colour'). A given note on the guitar will sound different (and therefore distinguishable) from the same pitched note on piano, violin, flute etc. There is usually also a difference in timbre from one guitar to another.

**Time signature** — a sign at the beginning of a piece which indicates, by means of figures, the number of beats per bar (top figure), and the type of note receiving one beat (bottom figure).

**Tone** — a distance of two frets; i.e. the equivalent of two semitones.

**Transposition** — the process of changing music from one key to another.

**Treble** — the upper regions of pitch in general.

**Treble clef** — a sign placed at the beginning of the staff to fix the pitch of the notes placed on it. The treble clef (also called 'G clef') is placed so that the second line indicates as G note.